This book is traumatic growth in action. Through vulnerability and honesty, this story highlights the warning signs, provides understanding and highlights resources for those in need. The author is fighting against the stigma of interpersonal violence and mental health, standing up saying that it is important to seek help and stick with it. An important read for professionals, victims, and those that love them.

Dr. Jennifer O'Donnell, PsyD

Everything we know about people who have experienced domestic and sexual assault, we have learned from their stories. Each story is unique and heartbreaking, and amazing. A Purpose Greater Than Sorrow is such a story. In it, Diann Diaz shares her long and painful and miraculous journey. Every time trauma attacked, she found her way back to life. She graces us with her resilience and hope.

Pat Brown – Executive Director of Women's Resource Center of the New River Valley, Inc. 1986-2019.

A Purpose Greater Than Sorrow is an inspiring and emotional journey through the author's experiences of rape and domestic violence and how she found her voice, strength, and true love to help her through those situations. The sensitivity yet candor with which she shares her experience will be a great value to survivors everywhere, helping them to know that they are not alone and inspiring them to find their own purpose.

Vanessa Kennedy, Advance Reader Review

A
PURPOSE
GREATER THAN
SORROW

Finding Courage After Sexual
Assault and Domestic Violence

DIANN DIAZ

This book is based on true events. To maintain anonymity, the author has changed some names of individuals.

This publication is designed to educate and provide general information regarding the subject matter based on the author's experience.

Edited by Kerry Genova, Writersresourceinc.com

Cover design by The Paper House Books Publishing Company

Text design by Lorna Reid

Photography by Beth Preston

ISBN: 978-1-7370439-0-4

Dedication

To all Victims and Survivors
And their loved ones

Life must be understood backward
[Although]…it must be lived forward.

Soren Kierkegaard

If I don't write, I will once again be silenced, just like the child-me; in essence, my uncle, again, will silence me. If I don't write my secrets, I will, in effect, still be keeping his. Only my own words can finally fill that blank, empty space that once was me.

Contents

✣

ABOUT THE AUTHOR xi

INTRODUCTION xiii

A WORD FROM MY HUSBAND, JOE xv

PART ONE - STOLEN CHILDHOOD xvii

CHAPTER 1

    Childhood Sexual Assault 1

CHAPTER 2

    Life at Home 15

CHAPTER 3

    Breaking my Silence 26

CHAPTER 4

    School 36

PART TWO - TURBULENT TIMES 49

CHAPTER 5

    Richard 51

CHAPTER 6

    Life after Divorce 64

CHAPTER 7

    Jim 77

CHAPTER 8

    Child Abuse 88

CHAPTER 9

    Life After Abuse 97

PART THREE - BETTER DAYS AHEAD 113

CHAPTER 10

Finding Happiness 115

CHAPTER 11

Public Speaking 128

CHAPTER 12

Changes & Losing Mom 136

CHAPTER 13

Women's Resource Center 146

CHAPTER 14

Emergency Advocacy 159

PART FOUR - MENTAL HEALTH AND THE ROAD TO HEALING 171

CHAPTER 15

Suicidal Ideation 173

CHAPTER 16

Depression 187

CHAPTER 17

Living for Today 199

EPILOGUE 204

ACKNOWLEDGMENTS 209

THANK YOU 211

TRAININGS 213

PRESENTATIONS of PERSONAL STORY 215

RESOURCES 217

DEFINITIONS 219

ABOUT THE AUTHOR

Diann Diaz lives in the Blue Ridge Mountains of Virginia with her husband and two dogs.

She was the Violence Prevention Educator, serving middle and high school students to prevent violence in relationships, helping them build healthy relationships, and informing them where to turn for help, and was proudly known for emergency advocacy in hospitals and police stations.

She was also called upon to speak at local colleges, universities, civic organizations, and churches about her personal story of abuse.

Locally, you may find Diann at conferences across the state of Virginia, speaking on topics such as *"Domestic Violence Victims – Why Do They Stay,"* as well as her personal story of abuse.

Nationally, Diann is on the speaker's bureau for **RAINN** (Rape, Abuse, Incest National Network). She is dedicated to educating others on having healthy relationships. Diann is committed to exploring all possibilities of prevention and awareness for victims, helping them find their way to becoming survivors, and leading a joyful life.

Diann is a former board member of the **Women's Resource Center,** Radford, VA (2006), a recipient of the "Speaker of the Year" award from **Women in Distress of Broward County**, Florida, Speakers Bureau (2003-2004), and served on the executive committee for the Gorham PTA, Gorham, ME (1994-1996), among other organizations. For almost twenty years, Diann has volunteered selflessly with nonprofit organizations for the improvement of various communities.

In her spare time, she enjoys writing, painting, traveling, and spending time with her grandchildren.

She is writing her next book, "*Domestic Violence Victims – Why Do They Stay*," which will be published October 2021.

INTRODUCTION

I'm telling my story so others will be able to learn from it. It is my mission to help victims of abuse to find their voice and speak out against the abuser. My mission is to help stop the cycle of abuse.

My story is meant to illustrate to friends and family of someone who has experienced domestic abuse or sexual assault that we need allies who will not judge us and will advocate for us. You are in a position to help your loved ones understand their options, which can include filing a police report, seeking an order of protection, developing a safety plan, sharing crisis hotlines and shelter phone numbers. Your job as an ally is to empower a victim to make their own decisions. As they do, they will be on the journey from victim to survivor.

And if you've been a victim or survivor of abuse, I stand with you. No one deserves to be treated the way you have been treated. It may seem impossible to believe, but there is a way forward.

There is hope for those who've experienced abuse.

There is purpose greater than the sorrow. I know this is true since I lived this story. I wrote this book knowing it is true for you too.

A WORD FROM MY HUSBAND, JOE

Diann's journey from victim to survivor of abuse and domestic violence she experienced before we married put our relationship to the test in ways I never could have imagined.

She was depressed, and although she tried to hide it, I could tell. As a law enforcement officer, I'd been trained to spot and deal with abuse situations. I did encourage her to get professional help, but she had always been taught that was a sign of weakness. For too long, she continued to try to figure out a solution on her own.

Those years were extremely difficult. One minute, I'd be enjoying her company. The next, she'd get very quiet, disappearing into her thoughts as she relived one incident or another. She had nightmares that were triggered by something she saw or heard. She continued to battle her demons on her own for many years, trying to find her own journey to peace.

I loved her and was committed to her journey of peace in life, wanting nothing more for her. I bided my time, hoping and praying that she would soon get the help I knew she so desperately needed.

Diann came to realize that she needed professional help if she was ever going to move out of the cycle of victimhood that defined so much of her life. It took her close to eleven years until she finally started seeing a psychologist. He started her on the road to healing.

She has become stronger and happier than ever before. Her lust for life has manifested itself in a more loving relationship with me but also with her family and friends. As an example, on one day out of the blue she stated, "How about a trip to Italy?" I didn't know where that came from but within the next few days we made reservations and we went to not only Italy but Spain and France also. We had a spectacular time. I felt like I had the woman I fell in love with back. We now take trips all around the world meeting people along the way and just having a great time.

Today she is vibrant, friendly, outgoing, and more loving than she has ever been. She can go places and feel safe in her surroundings and has learned what life is really all about.

We've now been married twenty-three years. We have a deep understanding of one another, and I'm grateful to see so much hope and life emerge from the darkness of those early years.

PART ONE

STOLEN CHILDHOOD

CHAPTER 1

Childhood Sexual Assault

I LEFT SATURDAY, JUNE 30, 1979, with butterflies in my stomach as I entered the big white plane. I went to the Midwest to visit my aunt's family. The flight itself was fun, as I was not a nervous passenger. I felt grown up to be making this trip by myself. My father thought since I was fourteen, I was old enough to make this trip on my own. It was a great opportunity to spend time with a part of my family I had never really gotten to know.

Uncle Sal, was my mother's brother-in-law, an approachable, middle-aged, handsome, dark-haired man who was attentive to children.

Sal relished that we kids gravitated toward him. I would later learn how he exploited our attention by looking at him as "Cool Uncle Sal." To him, he saw the attention of children enticing, no matter who the child was; his children, other people's children, or children he saw from afar. My uncle didn't care that he stole away someone's childhood, taking their innocence from them. He acted without a second thought – it was second nature to him. It was the core of who he was, a pedophile.

I didn't know then that those next few days would become paramount to building the foundation of a new life I would live. That life would take me down an ugly road. An anniversary that I would abhor. A day that should have been for celebration. However, all it did was give me a memory that would haunt me for the next thirty-two years. I was unable to spend the day without shedding a tear.

It was the Fourth of July. Music was playing, children laughing, food cooking on the grill, and adults in the backyard, talking. The aroma from the grill danced through the air while shrieking children jumped in the kiddy pool, tossing water balloons, putting smiles on the faces of young and old alike. This was a day of celebration—the children waiting for the sun to set and the fireworks to begin. My aunt and uncle had three daughters and two sons. My two eldest cousins had children of their own, which helped make this day jam-packed full of noise.

I was playing cars with my second cousin, off in the distance, when my uncle joined us. Sal was a special person to him. Aren't all grandpas? Grandpas are supposed to be joyous and make life seem as if there wasn't a care in the world, right? My uncle did this for everyone around; at least, it appeared that way to me.

My young cousin and I imagined a construction site with all the Tonka trucks and equipment. My uncle lowered himself to the ground and grabbed a Tonka. We all laughed as the construction crew we imagined had to call AAA because the vehicles were damaged from fallen construction debris.

Sal started grooming me that afternoon. He talked to me in a kind fashion, making small gestures, and gradually sat closer and closer, finding my comfort level. Am I standoffish, hesitant or easygoing? Sal was warm, gentle, smiled a lot, and he did not raise his voice. Occasionally, Sal would gently nudge my shoulder and gauge my reactions. I had no reason to think anything other than a child playing and having fun with family. I trusted him, and he knew it.

The evening came as the fireworks exploded in showers of red, white, and blue. I sat on the stoop in the back of the house, watching the fireworks with amazement and joy. Sal sat next to me, and we talked about sports, friends, and my love of horses. All the while, the other adults and children were about twenty-five yards in front of us near the barbecue on their camping chairs.

We continued to watch the fireworks as he put his arm around my shoulder. It seemed innocent enough, an uncle putting his arm around his niece to watch the fireworks together. Then his hand reached down, touching my right breast. I was paralyzed by fear. I couldn't speak. I was in a state of total confusion. I felt my face burn hot, increasing each second. *What is he doing? It feels wrong. Why aren't my feet moving? Where is my voice?* If anyone glanced our way, his hand would move back to my shoulder. Moments later, his hand would be back on my breast.

My heart never pounded so fast and hard in all of my young years. I believe I could actually hear my heart beating and definitely felt the pressure in my ears. Although I was only fourteen years old, I knew that his behavior was wrong, but I had no idea what to do. I was frozen with shock. His behavior continued throughout the evening until the fireworks ended.

I knew nothing about sex or sexual relations. We were not taught anything about sex in school or what to do in these situations. The only thing we learned in school was about taking care of our health and about our periods. Sex education had not yet made it into the school system, so I was oblivious to anything sexual.

I never said a word to Sal, and he quickly gauged my fear of him, and I wouldn't speak up. Again, part of his grooming process. I don't know why I didn't speak up. As I look back, I ask myself questions. Was it that I was too petrified and couldn't say no to an adult? Or was I in shock that an adult who I trusted and was entrusted with my care would do such a thing to me? All I know is I felt shocked, fear, and paralyzed to do or say anything.

After the fireworks ended, I went home with my

cousin Anita and her husband. I was relieved to get away from Sal's home. I didn't mention anything that happened to my cousin. That night, I didn't sleep well at all. When I did manage to fall asleep, I wet the bed, the first time I can remember doing that since I was a young child. I was filled with embarrassment and shame.

The next day, Anita drove me to Sal's house. She had to work, and since Sal was on vacation from his job at Anheuser-Busch, this is where I spent the day. I was not thrilled about it, but what could I say. Was I to say I would not go to his house? Wouldn't she wonder why I didn't want to go? After all, I was there to spend time with the family.

That morning, my aunt and two cousins went to work. So Sal and I were alone. We had breakfast, and then he decided it would be fun to play pool. Sal had a pool table in the basement, just as we had at home. We turned on the radio and played some cool tunes, such as *My Sharona* and *Knock on Wood*. After an hour, Sal insisted we take a break.

Sal sat on the couch and said, "Diann, come and sit here with me for a few minutes and relax."

I left the pool table and did what he said, and moved toward the couch. I sat down, hesitant to be near him. As I sat down, my heart started to race, and I felt it pound through my ears. What is he up to this time, I thought as he sat only inches away from me. There, the grooming process continued and would evolve into much more than the mere touching from the night before.

Sal looked at me and said, "You are an excellent pool player. How much have you played before?"

"Don't you know we have a pool table at home? I play all the time with Dad and my friends. I like it a lot. I think Dad lets me win, so I don't think I'm that good."

"Do you realize just how special you are to me, Diann? I'm so glad you came to visit us this year. You have grown to be a beautiful young woman. You are very sweet and smart." As he finished saying those words, Sal leaned into me and kissed me like an adult, right on the lips.

I'd kissed no one like this before. *Why on earth is this happening?* But I did nothing. I was frozen. No one was in the house to stop this behavior.

Tenderly, my uncle said to me, "Diann, don't you like me to kiss you? You are so pretty and need to be kissed. You are precious."

I felt trapped, like I had no choice or say in the matter. Never had I been so uncomfortable in the presence of an adult. I didn't know what to do. I was numb, and I could not think at all. I lost my voice. *Why? Why can't I move or speak?*

"Now it's time to take your pants off." *Why does he need to take my pants off? What is this all about?*

"I can't. I'm having my period. I just can't." *Wow, I spoke!*

Sal's voice suddenly changed from being sweet to being stern. 'You will take your pants off, and you'll do it now!" I shivered and obeyed.

He unzipped his pants and forced my head between his legs. I had no idea what to do. He instructed me with a tone I had never heard before. I felt his penis down my throat and thought I was going to throw up. I kept gagging. He kept forcing my head with his hand. *Why was he making me do this? This is my uncle. This isn't right. Where is my voice?*

"Now, come with me," he snarled.

The next thing I knew, he was leading me up the stairs to his bedroom. He had a rifle that was leaning up against the dresser. Even though he didn't immediately say anything to me about the rifle, I had immediate fear. To this day, I can still see the look in his eyes. It was like daggers piercing through my soul. He laid me on his bed and took my childhood away.

My mind was racing. I stared at the ceiling, pretending this wasn't happening. It hurt, it hurt badly. Every second of his movements brought more and more pain. I lay there in tears.

Then he was finished. Sal looked at me with a menacing glare and said, "You will never speak a word of this to anyone. Do you hear me, Diann? If you do, you see that rifle? I'm not afraid to use it."

That did it. My lips were sealed as if someone had put superglue on them. No one was going to know about this day. He quickly left the bed and got into the shower a few feet from the master bedroom. He left the bathroom door ajar, keeping a watchful eye on me from the shower.

I stayed on the bed, too frightened to even move. I was disoriented and tried to comprehend what happened. I didn't even know what to call it. I didn't even have a concept of sex. He called for me to join him in the shower. I cried to him to leave me alone. *I actually spoke! Where did that come from? But if I had spoken up yesterday, this never would have happened. This is my fault.*

The next day was July 6. I was scheduled to fly home the following day. Sal informed me, with my aunt in the room, "Diann! I think you should stay longer! We are having such a wonderful time with you. There are so many things we still have to show you here. If you leave now, you will miss out on so much. Call your dad and ask to stay at least another week."

I did as Sal instructed. I was in fear of him. I called my dad.

"Dad, can I stay another week?"

Dad asked quizzically, "Diann, you've been there almost a week now. Why do you want to stay longer?"

I hesitated. I wanted to throw up again. "They say there is so much more for me to see, and they want to take me to more places. Is that okay with you?"

The conversation was a blur. The next thing I knew, I was staying another week. I didn't want the extra week; I wanted to go home. Why did I allow Sal to make that decision for me? Why was I allowing him to control me after what he had done to me? I was scared out of my mind. So scared and alone. How was I going to survive another week with this monster who had taken so much from me? It was going to be a living hell.

For thirty-two years, fireworks had been a major trigger for me. Not wanting to celebrate this holiday, nor wanting to see the beautiful presentations in the sky.

The next week was a haze. I split my time bouncing from my cousin Anita's house and my aunt and uncle's house. My memories of the time spent with Anita, who was a handful of years older than me, are vague. I continued to wet the bed throughout my stay. I was embarrassed watching my cousin repeatedly removing the wet sheets from my bed and hanging them outside on the line to dry. I crawled into myself and hid. Why was I wetting the bed at fourteen? Anita and I never spoke of the bedwetting incidents.

My visit had some exciting moments. We went to see a major league baseball game. I believe it was the Cincinnati Reds. We went to amusement parks, the usual visitor stops, and shopping trips. And every chance Sal got, he would try to sneak a feel here and there. I tried as best as I could to keep my distance from him, but it wasn't always possible. I tried to enjoy myself during the times we were on these excursions, but I wasn't the same. The child in me was gone, gone forever. I felt as if I were only half a person. Was life supposed to be normal after what happened?

On a sunny afternoon, I found myself alone again with Sal at his house. We were playing pool again, and we actually played an entire game of pool this time. Although, the game was not without incident. Sal took every opportunity to walk past and rub himself up against me, touching and kissing me. I took every chance I got to position myself on the opposite side of the pool table from him. To this day, I still do this while playing pool. He used my innocence to take advantage of me and shattered my world.

On another occasion, we were playing pool when my aunt suddenly came home early from work. The basement had windows along the edge closest to the ceiling, which opened to the backyard. I watched my aunt's legs as she continually walked back and forth in front of the window. I prayed she would come into the house and join us in the basement to prevent Uncle Sal from any of his behaviors, but to no avail.

Another incident I recall is Sal and I drove to the store to pick up some items my aunt had requested. The drive to the store was five miles, and I was nervous the entire way. When we arrived, he did not park out front as would be expected. Instead, he drove to the rear, placed the car in park, leaned over, and started kissing and fondling me. I froze again. What is wrong with me, I kept thinking. *Why do I keep freezing during these times? Where is my voice?*

An older woman drove next to us in a small red car moments later. I will never forget the look upon her face. It was a look of disgust, but it seemed as if her eyes were piercing at me. A feeling of guilt and embarrassment came upon me. *Why should I feel guilty?* It would not be until many years later I would learn this was not my fault. My uncle then put the car in drive, drove to the front of the store, parked the car, and we headed in to shop. As we shopped, we both walked up and down the aisle as if nothing had happened. Could people tell by looking at my face what he had done to me? Did my uncle look guilty? I doubt it.

The day I'd been longing for finally came. It was time to pack my bags, get out of Dodge, and head home. Home. *Well, at least it's not here.* With my bags packed and settled in the Oldsmobile, the family all hopped in, and off to the airport we went.

There were tears when we parted at the airport. However, little did they know, mine were tears of joy.

***

I walked off the plane, head held low with my blue eyes never rising. My father met me in the terminal at the Boston airport. As soon as I approached Dad, he looked happy to see me, but I didn't want to look at him. My feelings and emotions were running wild. I felt shame. I felt betrayed. He let me stay that extra week.

I told him I had to go to the bathroom. I quickly glanced around, searching for what I hoped would save me. I did not want to break down in front of my father. I spotted the restroom and raced to get in. I reached for the sink and held on to the rim with my shaking hands, trying desperately to catch my breath. I could barely breathe. Without warning, the tears started uncontrollably flowing. They streamed down my face. I couldn't stop crying. My head was reeling. I ached from every nerve in my body. Pain I couldn't understand. My heart and soul began to purge the events from the prior two weeks, now that I had come face to face with my father, the one person who could have saved me and didn't.

But what did I know? I knew in my mind, the mind of a fourteen-year-old, knowing my father was not to blame, but yet, blaming him at the same time.

Women came and went, and no one appeared to care about the girl crying uncontrollably, looking as if she was hiding. What seemed even stranger was my father had not even asked anyone to check on his daughter. Finally composed, I left the restroom after fifteen minutes. I found my father and went to retrieve my bags at baggage claim. As we walked to get my bags, I felt my legs buckle. *Can he tell what happened with Uncle Sal? Is he going to be mad with me?* I felt people staring, and I wondered if they could tell my innocence was taken from me. The seemingly endless thoughts flowing through my mind lost and horrified me. Now, we had over two hours of driving before we reached our home. *Oh, joy*!

We drove north along I-95, heading for home. As we departed the Boston area, I stared through the car window in silence. I was lost in thought, watching out the window as we drove past all the foliage. The drive took us from Massachusetts through New Hampshire and finally into Maine for the final forty-five minutes. Not a word was spoken between us. My father never asked about my trip, did I have fun, did I enjoy seeing the family. No, he didn't ask. I wanted to scream the words, but they were stuck, consumed by my fear.

My father never asked what happened at the airport. Me, his daughter, rushes off to the restroom. I came out, and it was obvious that I had been crying. I sat there in the passenger seat, praying he would break the deafening silence and ask me something.

I was bursting to talk to my father. I wanted to pour my heart out to him and tell him that my childhood had been ripped from me. *Dad, Uncle Sal raped me*…it petrified me to start the conversation. How could my father not see what was wrong, that his little girl was hurting? Why didn't my father want to know what was wrong? Did he love me? Did he care? Why didn't he ask?

Finally, we arrived home. We pulled into the driveway, and I thought home would never be the same; I felt paralyzed. As I was about to enter the house, I stopped for a moment. I paused there and pondered. I wasn't able to speak to my father about my trip; how was I going to speak to anyone else about it, especially the rest of my family. Oh. My. God.

I didn't want to enter the house. I felt sick and disgusted, but mostly I was ashamed. How could I face my family, my friends, life? I pulled myself together for that final push and went in.

I am home, finally away from that monster who took away my childhood. But I'm not the same. What will life be like now?

CHAPTER 2

Life at Home

I GREW UP IN a small town along the outskirts of Portland, Maine, from the age of seven until seventeen. A quiet, sleepy town where most everyone knew everyone.

I lived there with my parents, George and Catherine, along with my two brothers, Stephen, nine years older, and Guy, two years older. We were affluent or rich by others' description, but not filthy rich. Dad provided for the family well. Others likely saw us as the all-American family, but what lies behind closed doors is never seen by others.

Typically, Dad would be home for dinner by six. Throughout dinner, we often discussed our school day. Dad would continually remind us how important it was to keep good grades. He would ask us what homework we had that evening and prompt my brother Guy and me to show him. He was always stern with us to acquire top grades in school. He was demanding in his expectations. Those expectations raised my anxiety. I was nervous every night when I had to hand him my homework to be gone over with a fine-tooth comb. I wanted to live up to his expectations. When I failed, it overwhelmed me, and I didn't know where to place those feelings.

Dad was also known for saying, "stifle it" if one was to express themselves in any manner that was not to his liking, or if one of us kids, or Mom, were arguing. This was his way to tell us to cease.

My mom suffered from depression. One of the reasons for her depression was she lost her first daughter Cynthia to the court system before I was born. Mom was a heavy drinker. She would start drinking Miller Lites at noon on weekends and drink throughout the day. On weekdays, she would start when she got home from work, right before my brother and I returned from school and would drink until bedtime. Drowning her pain and anguish daily. This was her existence.

While I was growing up, it was never spoken of, but her actions were undeniable. Not that she was a falling down drunk; she functioned well enough to carry out what she needed to do each day. Whether she had cleaning to do or taking us to various places we needed to go, she did it. Thinking about it years later, the thought of how volatile she was and her driving us in her condition brings me chills. I suppose as a child you don't think of those types of things, nor should you have to. It wasn't until my teen years that her drinking became an issue for me.

Between my mother's drinking and her depression, it often led to chaos in the home. Each night, or so it seemed, there would likely be an argument between my father and her. During these times, my brother Guy and I would sit at the top of the stairs, listening to what they were arguing about, while I hugged my doll Kirsten tightly. Mom would yell, "George, you are always on Diann's side, when most of the time it's her fault. You discipline Guy when it should be Diann."

The funny thing was, she was right; it was her approach that was horrific. Arguing would persist, then there would be silence, and you could hear Mom's bedroom door slam. Dad? He would stay downstairs, watching TV in the living room for a short period of time. Guy and I would rush to our rooms. Shortly thereafter, we would hear Dad come up the stairs and go into his bedroom.

My parents argued incessantly. Not a single day went by that my mother was not raising her voice at my father. Mom would be seething with anger, spewing unimaginable language at my father and throwing things. I never saw my parents physically abuse each other. It was more psychological warfare and verbal abuse.

My parent's continual arguing was mostly about us, the kids. I kept my head low at home, hoping to stay out of the line of fire. My friends at school had no idea of what I was enduring at home. How could they possibly know? How could they have even a hint? I was such a social butterfly at school, and I loved people and always appeared happy. I loved the attention I received from them.

Whenever we would have company at the house, whether it was for birthdays, Thanksgiving, Christmas, or even friends coming over to hang out, no one would even realize the chaos that would normally take place in our home. It looked as if Mom was the "Stepford Wife." It appeared like the perfect little household. That always seemed odd to me how Mom would change when others were around. I always loved it when we had company.

Understand, my father did not know how to show affection physically or verbally. He never used his words. His answer for affection was to buy me things. All my life, my family and friends always commented that I was "Daddy's little girl." Some would say he spoiled me, and I suppose he did by the things he bought. All I had to do was ask. But I didn't feel loved. "Things" never satisfied me. Not that I wasn't thankful. It was out of a daily basis of not having a hug or hearing "I love you." I never felt I was good enough in his eyes.

At nine years old, I told my dad, "I want a horse." How did he respond?

"Okay, Diann, but you have to take riding lessons

and learn how to take care of them for a year before you can have one."

Simple as that. I took riding lessons, learned how to take care of a horse, and bada bing, a year later, I had a horse!

That was my life, basically. Anything I wanted, I got. Nothing seemed out of the question for Daddy's little girl.

Life certainly could have been worse, and I know that. However, I would have given back all the horses, bikes, toys, summer camps just to have been fortunate enough to have had parents who would listen to me and tell me they love me. Instead, he bought me things. That was the only way he knew how. But I didn't realize that when I was a little girl.

**

After my return from my uncle's house, I was not the same carefree, social butterfly that had left to spend what was to be a fun-filled vacation with family. I felt different, and I was good at hiding it from my friends. To them, nothing had changed, so I thought. I didn't have any respect for my parents. I didn't try to show any. I was hurting and lashing out. I would yell and swear. Something I had never dared to do before. My tone was loud, and I would spew every hurtful word I could think of. This was not my behavior before my trip. I had changed over those two weeks.

My father felt the brunt of my angst. I acted as if he had traumatized me instead of Sal. Had he? Was I reacting to his ambivalence to my behavior changes? He never said one word about the change in my attitude since returning from the trip, never even questioned it. Had they not noticed? How could they not?

I was never detained, spoken to, yelled at, nothing. It was as if it never happened. I had blasted them with four-letter words I had never used before, although learned from my mother. These words coming out of my young mouth had to have been as surprising to them as they were for me. But never once had it occurred to them to ask me what was wrong.

I was on my way upstairs one night, and when Dad asked me to do something, I screamed, "F--- you, Dad." He stood frozen, never saying a word. I stood there staring at him for what seemed like forever. Honestly, I think my hatred of everything that had happened to me, the fact no one had cared enough to "save" me, was boiling within me, and the percolator inside me blew. I'd never spoken to anyone that way before, especially not my father. I continued up the stairs to my room, slammed the door, and cried myself to sleep.

I was conflicted and confused. I felt as if I were trapped in a continuous loop of a nightmare, but this was no ordinary nightmare. However, it was my reality, my living hell. As if I had gone to sleep one day and had woken up in a world totally foreign to me. Who was I? What was happening to me? What had happened to the child I was before that fateful trip? I hated my life; I hated myself. Only going to school and being with my friends gave me a reprieve from the constant self-loathing and the shattered world that I was now living in. I did everything I could to become a teacher's pet. In so doing, I would receive the attention I desperately sought. Every day was a performance. I couldn't wait for school to start in the fall.

***

Danny and I met on July 28, 1979, at a mutual friend's party that was held at Wassamski Springs in Scarborough. It is a family campground with a one-mile sandy beach on a private lake. I was there with Susan H. and her family, having a wonderful time. I certainly needed time away from my house. This was just weeks after my rape, and I needed to be with friends. As the day progressed, I kept viewing this one guy who was talking to Susan's boyfriend. As I was checking him out, I thought, hmm…I'll have to ask Susan to introduce me since she must know him! Introductions were soon made. After meeting Danny, my smile didn't leave my face for the rest of the day.

All of us hanging out were teenagers and some in their twenties. People were having fun, drinking from the keg. Looking back, I think Susan and I were probably the youngest. I'd never had alcohol before. Someone handed me the first cup of beer I would ever have in my life. I didn't hesitate to accept it. I quickly drank it, hoping it would numb the feelings inside. This time during my life, I didn't care what I was doing. I had no respect for myself at all. I felt damaged, so why not.

My dad forbade me from dating Danny once he learned he was seventeen. I went behind my dad's back and would meet up with Danny when I went to a friend's house. I wasn't going to allow my parents to stop me from seeing him. At that age, I was rebelling against everything and everyone. My parents had no idea I was going to see him when I would go to Susan's house, along with others from school. I had my mom take me to disco clubs, where Danny would meet up with me. Mom knew Danny would be there but kept that information from Dad.

It was September, and fall was in the air, keeping the secrets of what winter weather we could expect. It should have been a time full of joy with the expectation of the upcoming holidays. But that was not to be.

This was the time that my mother, for the first time in my recollection, spoke to me instead of at me. Mom informed me my father was moving out, and they were divorcing. She actually appeared happy for once. She welcomed the divorce as if a great weight had been lifted from her shoulders.

There must have been love and happiness between them at some point. It seems sad to say I don't remember those times. They may have been happy when I was young, or maybe it was an illusion. What can you say about two people who are married for seventeen years, living separate lives, never sharing a bedroom, and verbally destroying each other every day? You could say they are two unhappy people that should not be together. I truly believe they were only together because of us, the kids. No other reason comes to mind.

I was relieved after my mom told me about the divorce. It felt strange having my father living in our house after the rape. I was Daddy's little girl for so long, but now I was damaged. He hadn't protected me. He hadn't asked what had happened. Was he going to do to me what Sal had done to me? I was afraid. I felt unwanted and unnoticed. *Why doesn't anyone ask me what is wrong and help me? But most importantly, why doesn't my father care?*

Because of the divorce, we had to move. Our new house was on a standard home lot, and therefore, did not have sufficient land to house my horse. "Diann, we'll find a new home for Mama." The words were driven through my heart like spears, leaving a gaping hole there. Of course, why not? Everything else is going to hell, I thought to myself.

For at least a week, I cried myself to sleep. I was losing my horse, my best friend in the world. Not only my best friend but my confidant, savior, the one I could always count on to ease the burning pain that existed within me. The day came when Mama was sold. I knew it was going to happen; I just didn't know when.

One morning, I got up and fed Mama as I did every day. I left for school, not knowing what awaited me. When I returned home, Mama was gone. No goodbyes, no, "Diann, Mama will not be here when you get home." Neither Mom nor Dad had said anything to me. Nothing. It was as if selling my best friend was like throwing out the trash. Not one iota of thought of how I would feel. I felt sick, devastated, and alone.

The day Dad moved out was an interesting one. I went to school like any other day, and when I got home, all his personal items were gone. We didn't see him leave; he was just gone. It was like what had occurred with Mama. They tell you it's going to happen, but not when. In hindsight, I should have known. The prior evening, Dad sat Guy and me down, telling us he was moving to Scarborough. It wasn't far from where we lived. He said we could come visit him anytime we wanted, and he would visit us on Wednesday nights after dinner. With that, the conversation was over. Quick, sweet, and to the point, like my father usually was. Dad's townhouse suited him well. He seemed happy, at least happier than I remember seeing him in a long time.

Soon after Dad left, our house quickly sold. We moved into our new house. It was a blue ranch styled home with three bedrooms. The house was closer to our schools. Now it was just Mom, Guy, and me.

Stephen had been in the army for five years now. With all the tumultuous changes this year had brought, there was more still awaiting our arrival.

What a year 1979 was turning out to be. Little did I know there was more to come.

CHAPTER 3

Breaking my Silence

IN OUR NEW HOME, there were no rules but a lack of respect. The only thing my brother and I were responsible for was school. Other than that, we had free rein in our lives.

Mom had a good job, cooked us meals, kept a clean house, and was a partier. Danny and I went out on dates since Dad wasn't there to stop me. There was no way I was going to let either of my parents tell me to break up with him. Hell, they weren't trying to help me regarding the incident with my uncle. *Why am I going to let them take away someone who is good to me? Screw them!* That was my attitude.

Dad would come over once a week on Wednesdays and thoroughly examine my homework assignments. It was now my freshman year of high school. My brother, since he was a senior, got a free pass on being scrutinized regarding his homework. He didn't need anyone on his back. He was an "A" student most of his life. Dad trusted him.

At first, it seemed strange to have Dad coming to the house since he didn't live with us anymore. But if it made him uncomfortable, he never showed it. Dad would sit with me at the kitchen table, the table that was no longer his, for about an hour helping me with my math homework.

"Diann, what have you been working on in math this week? Any problems?"

I didn't even want to answer him, as I knew it would become a big issue going over the chapter in my workbook.

"We are just learning about Algebra, Dad. We haven't begun much at all."

Well, that's all he needed to hear. He opened up my math book, and we sat for an hour and a half while he instructed me on math problems that had yet to be assigned. I was lost!

While insisting on my excelling in school, I felt the pressure. He would grill me with math problems, and I would feel my anxiety level rise; it rose to a level that made me want to escape. I felt trapped. No wonder it never stuck!

Eventually, I started taking advantage of the "no rules" policy at home. Mom would go out partying at night with her friends from work. That left Guy and me to do whatever our little hearts desired. One night while Mom was out, I took a bottle of rum. I got on my bike and headed to the cemetery a half-mile from the house. I sat there in the dark and drank half the bottle. Wash away the pain? Why not? Damn it! I lived in a body of such pain and secrets.

It was after midnight when I finally returned home. My brother Guy saw me enter the house but never said a word. He just turned away and proceeded to his room. I believe he was worried about me, but he would never admit it. He was most likely just happy I returned safely, although I was drunk.

Being a partier, my mother eventually took me partying with her. A fourteen-year-old child, out partying at bars with my mother, even on school nights. I don't know what she was thinking by doing this. Did she not want me going out alone at night? She always had me dance with guys she liked. What did I know? I was having fun with Mom. Finally, having fun with Mom. This way?

On any given night, we would enter the Holiday Inn in Westbrook, around seven. We both would typically wear jeans with a nice blouse or sweater. Mom was always wearing her leather jacket. I wasn't even wearing makeup yet. As soon as we entered the hotel, we'd make a left and down the hall to the bar area. Many people there instantly recognized us, and most would say hello. Mom and I always looked for a table close to the dance floor to watch the band. We were there so often that we knew most of the bands that played at the bar.

Mom would ask, "Diann, you want your Diet

Coke, right?" I would answer her, and she'd head right for the bar. She'd return with her beer and my soda, plus a shot of rum, which she would pour into my glass. Of course, at my age, I thought this was pretty cool.

One regular, Bumpin' Bill, would come ask me to dance. I danced with him since I knew him and felt safe. My mother and her girlfriends would scope out the place for guys, any guys. She'd spot some random men, make eye contact, and it wasn't long before two or three would sit at our table, buying rounds of drinks.

My mother was a brazen woman, and it would show even more when she drank. She would look over at one man then say, "Ask my daughter to dance. She would love to dance with you."

I'd be embarrassed and say, "MOM!" She would just throw daggers at me with her stare. Of course, I went up and danced with a stranger so I would not piss my mother off. Nothing worse than having my mother drunk AND pissed off!

After the song ended, back to my seat I would go. Still embarrassed. My mother, she'd be happy as a pig in a sty. She'd give me a smile and a nod. Because the guy would sit closer to her, and that made her happy. As I look back, it seems as if she was using me as bait to lure men for her. We would dance the night away, but at closing time, the night was still young.

"Hey, everyone come back to my house, and I'll

cook you up some breakfast," my mother would frequently say on evenings we went out.

Many times, men came back to the house, and the partying would continue. Some of these men were "attracted" to me. I had fun with the attention, but not with the actions they made toward me. They would flirt and reach out to touch me. I would look sternly and back up every time. Because these men were drunk, they didn't take notice of my rejection. It wasn't long before I would give up and go to bed. And this all happened with my mother present. It didn't faze her. She didn't care.

Typically, when we all got to the house, I went to bed, as I had school in the morning. From my blue-painted bedroom with pictures of horses on the wall, I could hear the adults laughing and carrying on. My room was just outside the kitchen.

One particular night, things almost got out of hand. My mother showed her true colors. I had gone to bed since I had school the next morning. I could hear them still partying when suddenly, a drunk, staggering man came into my room. He leaned over and tried to kiss me and fondle me. The scent of the liquor and his body stench permeated the room, and the odor was almost suffocating.

I yelled, "Get the hell out of here!"

I then reached over the side of my bed and grabbed a golf club that I kept there just in case something like this were to happen. I had stolen the club from my brother weeks ago. Then I swung the club and hit him over the head with it. He left my room. I was proud of myself. I fought back. I was finally standing up for myself. The next thing I know, my mother comes running into my bedroom. She was livid.

"Why did you do that to him?" Mom yelled accusingly.

"Mom, he was reaching down to kiss me while I was sleeping. And he tried to touch me where he shouldn't be," I yelled back.

"Well, you shouldn't have done that. Now they are all leaving."

Yes, that's my mother. More upset these "gentlemen" were leaving the house than her daughter being mauled by a drunk. She was *pissed*. How dare I do such a thing? Oh boy. God forbid I take care of myself and not get raped again, I thought. I turned over and cried.

***

We were living in our new home for a few months, and I struggled with whether or not to tell my parents about the rape. I didn't know what to say, how to say it, and worse yet, I had no idea how they would react. I ached to release the burden I had been carrying for months. I waited for one of my father's Wednesday visits.

"Mom, Dad, I have something to tell you."

They both sat down at the opposite end of the

table and looked at me intently, and were silent. I stood at the table, my body shaking and feeling as if I would vomit. I knew this was the time, the time to break my silence. I bolted with the words.

"I wanted to let you know Uncle Sal raped me on my trip last summer."

I distinctly remember my father repeating my uncle's name as a question. I replied, "Yes."

There was a deafening silence in the room, when abruptly and without warning, my father grabbed his jacket and stormed from the house.

My mother's only response to me was, "Well now, see what you've started."

Shock. Disillusionment. Anger. I didn't know what to make of what had happened. This pain was worse than the rape. No sympathy, no hugs, no telling me it wasn't my fault. Nothing. It was almost as if reliving being traumatized all over again.

Why did my mother allow me to travel halfway across the country and stay at a sex offender's home? (A few years later, I found out she knew of his behaviors, as he had done the same to others, but she still let me go on that trip.) Why did my father leave the house without a word? I felt worthless. No one cared. No one loved me. That's how I felt. How can parents do that to a child? Maybe they did not know what to say, but to me, they are only thinking of themselves, not their child. Couldn't they have at least consoled me? Tell me they love me?

In school the previous year, I was a straight-A student, riding my horse, listening to music in my room, going roller-skating with my friends, and was respectful to my parents. Now I was drinking heavily. I did what I wanted when I wanted. I became verbally abusive to both of them. In this respect, I can say that I had a skilled teacher—my mother.

I was still dating Danny and going to his house on a regular basis. Danny's family home was an older two-story home. The house always smelled fresh, as if his mother had lilies and daffodils in every room. Each time I arrived at their home, his family gave me such a warm, welcoming reception and always with big smiles. Oh, what a wonderful feeling! Their presence was exhilarating. To breathe the air in their home was refreshing. There was no yelling, screaming, no chaos. I soaked in their family love. I had that. I had them. Thank God.

***

On a cold, breezy Sunday, the week Christmas break was starting, Dad and I went ice skating in Portland. We skated for an hour, having an enjoyable time when Dad mentioned he wanted to discuss something with me.

We sat on the cold stone bench, chilled, even with our scarfs and mittens. Dad said, "There is a boarding school an hour away, and I'd like to talk to you about it."

I sat quietly, letting him speak.

"The class sizes are very small, so you would get more attention from the teachers. The school has many sports available. Downhill skiing, swimming, hockey, lacrosse, and more. You'd be living with a roommate, and, of course, you'd be coming home for spring break."

He was selling it like a used car salesperson trying to dump an old clunker. He looked at me matter-of-factly. I sensed he had a bit of fear I wouldn't agree with going to the school, or he would have a hard time convincing me to go.

"Dad, why do you want me to go to this school? It sounds as if you really want me to go," I said to him with hesitation.

"Well, Diann, I think with your current living situation, it's best to get you somewhere else, and I also think this school has better studies for you than your public school."

We continued to discuss it at length, and eventually, I agreed. In thinking back, I don't think I ever disagreed with much of anything my father said I was to do. Since informing him of the situation that took place the past summer, I was more at ease with him, as he did talk to me with more kindness.

I believe my father had two reasons he wanted to send me to this school. First, to get me away from my mother and all her destructive influences. As you have surmised by now, my mother was a handful. And second, was for a change of scenery, specifically to get me away from Danny.

After our discussion, it was set. After Christmas break, I would move into the boarding school. No more friends to see at my public school. I wouldn't even have a chance to say goodbye to them. That's all too familiar.

CHAPTER 4

School

THE SCHOOL'S CAMPUS WAS idyllic. It lies in the forest and hills on the eastern edge of the White Mountains, near the ski resort where I learned to ski. The campus itself was comprised of many red brick buildings and large areas of green space. The student population was small, between 200-300 students, and included international students. It was a mixture of sixth grade through postgraduate studies. Only freshman through postgrads were boarded. However, boarding was optional.

January 1980, during the second half of my freshman year of high school, my parents transferred me to this private coed boarding school. Once again, my life was changing. I was taken away from my friends at public school, and I felt abandoned. My parents sent me away to deal with the pain alone. I felt as if no one cared about me, and I continued not having support.

My roommate was so much fun. Aglae was from Spain, spoke English well with a heavy accent. She had long dark hair with the most gorgeous brown eyes. She was a barrel of laughs. We would stay up to all hours of the night talking, laughing, and sometimes even crying about stories we shared. It was a wonderful friendship. Even though she was from another country and I was from a small town in Maine, our different languages and cultures didn't affect either of us. But I never told her about the rape. I never felt safe enough to share.

For the past five months at home, I didn't have to worry about any consequences for my actions. I stayed out late, smoked cigarettes, drank alcohol, and even smoked a little weed now and then. I was easing my pain. Maybe that was one of the reasons my father sent me here, to receive some authority and guidance in my life. Either way, now I had to get used to following rules. In by ten, lights out at eleven. No drinking, no smoking. No excuses.

Little did he know…

Before long, as with many kids, I found ways around the rules. It didn't take much time before I was smoking marijuana almost every day. I smoked in the afternoon after classes. I was depressed as a repercussion of the rape, and I also believe because of the abandonment I felt from my parents, that smoking was one of my escapes. I would sometimes sit in my room alone, smoking a joint, blowing the smoke out the window while playing Crosby, Stills, Nash, and Young on my 8-track tape and chill, trying not to think of the pain that Uncle Sal had caused. It would help for only a short time.

I had continuous feelings of sadness and hopelessness. I felt guilt and worthlessness. It appeared I was happy, as I had friends and interacted with them. I went to my classes and did well with my studies. I had a mixture of emotions, and I hid my feelings.

At night as I lay in bed trying to go to sleep, the memories of Sal would creep in and prevent me from a restful night.

While in classes, I paid attention, learned what I had to learn and passed my tests, but at night it was a chore to do my homework. I felt robotic day in and day out. It was a learned behavior to do well from the pressure of my father. I suppose that was a good thing, as it kept me from thinking of Uncle Sal during my classes. But after class, that was a different story.

If I didn't go back to my room to smoke my weed, I'd go to this particular building on campus. It had a room in the basement where many students would hang out. The postgraduates supplied beer, and we would drink or get high. I was exposed to drugs I had never even heard of at the time. There was heroin, cocaine, black beauties, and many others. I have no idea where they came from. I am thankful I never touched any of these, but the exposure was something I'll never forget. Something I don't think my father would have appreciated!

***

A friend of mine from class informed me a specific teacher was one person to buy marijuana from on campus. From that point forward, I would always buy marijuana from him instead of one of the postgraduates.

It was a cloudy Monday afternoon when classes were complete when I met up with Mr. O'Connor in his apartment. Like the entire faculty, he was living in a dorm room at the end of the hall as a dorm parent. I knocked on his door. He let me in with that gorgeous smile.

"How are your studies going, Diann?" I chuckled to myself as he was asking about my schoolwork while I was there to buy marijuana. I thought that was comical.

"Going well. I think I could do better in history. I can't stand that class, but it is what it is."

"Here is a dime bag." I handed him ten dollars, thanked him, and went on my way. As I was leaving his building, all I could think was, "What would my father think of me spending his money on pot."

I saw this teacher every day in class, plus I was buying my weed from him, so we interacted regularly. I ended up having a big crush on him, one that many girls my age would have on one of their teachers. At that age, it seemed to me the feelings were mutual. It ended with me in a precarious situation with him.

He invited me to his room one day in the dorm. I thought to buy weed. Little did I know then what was about to happen. When I got to his room, we talked about school, we flirted, and we ended up having sex. I didn't say no. I didn't say yes. It just happened. I was only fifteen; he was twenty-eight and paid attention to me. As far as I knew, it was okay since I didn't say no. I wanted to have someone care about me. He didn't care about me; he just wanted some action. Years later, I came to realize what he did was illegal. He was a teacher first and foremost; I was fifteen, and he was an adult, and my parents had placed their trust in him and the school. What he did to me was not okay. It was illegal, as was the selling of marijuana.

The rest of the semester, his behavior toward me changed. Although my puppy love had grown, his demeanor toward me had turned cold and indifferent. I'm sure he did not want any of the other teachers/professors on campus to find out, so he kept his distance from me, except for selling me marijuana, of course. I also became acutely aware there were other girls whose interactions with him were like mine. I can only imagine how many others were in the same position I was in.

***

Throughout the semester, there were visits from Danny. I loved Danny's visits. He was my one connection to my real life. I felt this life I was leading here at school was beyond comprehension. I would show him around campus, and we'd picnic on the lawn near the football field. We'd talk about school, and he'd tell me what was going on with our friends. The friends I longed to see. Since he was now a senior, we spoke about the prom, which was right around the corner. When he asked me to go, I was thrilled. Since my school would be finished by the end of May, I would be home in time to attend. This gave me something to look forward to. I needed something positive in my life, and Danny was always one to supply.

May was the end of the semester, and considering all that had occurred, I did pretty well with my grades. Now it was time to go home for the summer. I, however, had other ideas about school for the fall. I did not want to return for my sophomore year.

When Dad came to pick me up to head home for the summer, we loaded the car with all my belongings. When we were driving away, I said, "Dad, I don't want to come back next year. I want to go back to public school in the fall." His face was staring sternly at the road. His hands clinging to the wheel.

"Why's that?"

"Well, I'm away from my friends. I don't really need to be here, Dad." As I informed him, my stomach was knotting up, and I could feel my hands getting sweaty.

"Let me think about it."

With those words, my heart dropped. I felt I was doomed to go back.

If he only knew about the sex and drugs that went on at this boarding school that he obviously paid a lot of money for, he'd do more than cringe. Although from his past responses in what had occurred in my life, would he?

School year over, and summer began. Life went back to usual living at Mom's house. The partying, the bars, the men. If it weren't for Danny during that time in my life, I don't know where I'd be today. Would I have been just another statistic? He and his parents were my saving grace. They may not have known it, but I hope I showed my appreciation to them as often as I was in their presence.

Thankfully, Dad approved my staying with Mom and attending the local high school once again.

My sophomore year consisted of still going out with Mom to the bars. That didn't stop. I did, however, still think it was cool. I could drink with my mother at my age, but I didn't think it was cool to be mauled by the men she met. It only emphasized the fact just how many men were like Uncle Sal.

Danny and I would go to plenty of parties in town with our friends, and Mom would allow me to have keg parties at the house. She would party right along with us. My friends all seemed to think it was cool. Guy was there, and he'd invite his friends too.

The house was always full of teenagers having a good time.

My friends had no idea what my life was like. They thought my life was great. Sure, Mom would let me have keg parties, then I'd find her in bed with one of my friends. Or be upset with me when one of her friends made the moves on me, and I was not appreciative. Not a part of life I liked, nor one I wanted to live. No one knew the "behind the scenes." And there was much more, much, much more than that. Misery. Pain. Unsupported. Such a blank existence.

***

My mother's cruelty knew no bounds. You see, my mother would allow my uncle to come to our house any time he and his family came to town. She didn't concern herself with how that would make me feel. She was only worried about not wanting to make a "scene" or "upset" anyone in the family. What was I, chopped liver?

I heard the knock at the door while hiding in my room. My mother greeted my aunt and uncle with open arms. "Welcome! Come on in, Sis!" Ugh, then I'd hear his voice.

"Hello, Catherine. How have you been?" Uncle Sal inquired as he entered the house. My blood had boiled by now.

"Where are the kids?" he asked curiously.

"I'm doing great! Diann is in her room, and Guy

is at the golf course." It was bad enough this rapist was in our house. Now she had to add insult to injury.

"Diann, won't you come out here, please?" As I came out of my room, it was all I could do to even look at my uncle. I glanced at my aunt and said hello. I felt my anxiety rising. I didn't want to be put in this position. I didn't want to be here. Why are they here? Why has my mother allowed *him* to be here? With a lot of trepidation, I hesitated and gave a quick glance to my uncle, said hello, and let my eyes quickly moved to the floor.

"Mom, I'm going over to Danny's house for a while. His mother is having a surprise dinner for his father, and I don't want to miss it." This was a lie, but off the top of my head, it's all I could think of.

"Diann, we have company, and I don't want you leaving. We will head to Grampie's house shortly, and I thought you would like to go," Mom snapped.

"Sorry, Mom, I'm going to Danny's."

And that was all that was said, and I grabbed my brown pocketbook and headed out the door. How in the world did she expect me to stay there? I never quite knew how or why she expected me to be in the same room with this man.

***

During my junior year, I learned there was a college nearby that high school students could attend while still in high school. This piqued my interest. My grades weren't bad, but they weren't the best either. I had mostly As and Bs with an occasional C. I hoped they would be "good enough." I knew if I was accepted, I would live on campus in Portland, even though we only lived twenty minutes away. At least I wouldn't be in Mom's house. Things had not gotten any better at home, and I wanted to get out. Deep down inside, I believe I knew how toxic her environment was.

I was elated at the concept of going to college a year early. To me, it would be an accomplishment. Not only getting out of Mom's house as my decision but also something I hoped my father would be proud of. I still felt the need to excel in his eyes.

I went to my guidance counselor's office and obtained all the necessary paperwork that I would need. I discussed it with my father one Wednesday evening. He thought this to be a wonderful idea. The submission papers were sent, and I was accepted. In August, I would be a freshman in college living on campus while still being considered a senior in high school.

***

Danny and I continued dating throughout high school. There were a few times we broke up, but those times never lasted long. We'd break up for a couple of weeks. I dated Brad for a few weeks, then got back together again with Danny. When it came time for me to go to college, we ended the relationship. However, while in college, we dated a few times. He will always be in my heart, and I will always be grateful for the trust and support I received from him and his family. He was the first sounding board and support system I had after the rape, and I was fortunate to have been with him. He was gentle, patient, listened, and genuinely cared about how I felt. He never tried to take advantage of me, and that is what I believe my parents thought he was doing, as he was older than I was. He and his family were just what I needed at that time in my life. They proved to me that there were good people in this world, and I needed to know that.

My first year of a two-year program at college was a lot more fun than I had expected. I had a great group of girls in my dorm. We, of course, had parties, but not the type of parties I was used to with my mother and men at her house. We played music and danced, and yes, there was drinking, but it never got out of hand. There were lots of smiles for everyone. I was only seventeen, which was a year younger than most of the students.

I was studious and made it a point to keep my grades up. I spoke to my father on the phone once a week. He always wanted to catch up with me and my studies. He seemed pleased with me, and that's what I yearned for. He was living in Costa Rica six months out of the year now, so the phone calls were his way of keeping in touch.

After my first year, I was able to graduate with my high school class, and I went to the prom again with

Danny. I felt left out not being there my senior year, as that is an important year for anyone in high school, but trust me, it honestly was worth it to me to not be at home.

The second year started like the first—lots of great friends, studying, and good times. When it was time for the Halloween party, there was a security guard that caught my attention. He was standing in the halls, making sure nothing got out of hand. I glanced at him many times. I got up the nerve about an hour into the party and walked up to him and asked him his name.

"Hey there. Looks like everything is under control here. You look a little bored. What's your name?"

"Dick. And yes, you guys are pretty good here. I'm not expecting any problems. Go have fun. We'll talk later."

I was a little disappointed he didn't want to talk more, but I suppose to him, it wouldn't look good fraternizing with a student for any length of time. Boy, he sure was good-looking. Tall, dark, and handsome would be an understatement! If I had anything to do with it, I was definitely going to get more attention from him.

A month later, I saw him again on campus, and he asked me out for a drink. Of course, I said yes; it flattered me. This guy is adorable! I later found out he was thirteen years my senior.

We had a fun first date. We went to a Chinese restaurant for dinner and drinks and laughed the night away. A red light should have popped into my head when he informed me I needed to give him a ride home. He didn't own a car, and he lived at the YMCA.

A few weeks later, Guy and I visited Dad in Costa Rica to celebrate New Year's. When I returned a week later, Dick asked me out again. We continued dating until April, when he then popped the ultimate question. We were engaged. Our relationship had progressed too quickly.

PART TWO

TURBULENT TIMES

CHAPTER 5

Richard

On May 9, 1984, Dick and I drove to a white farmhouse in Westbrook, Maine. This is where the city clerk lived and where the wedding ceremony was to take place. I never informed my parents of what was about to happen. I felt they would try to talk me out of this decision. I didn't want to hear it.

We entered the old-style home, fashioned with antique furniture. The clerk informed us where to stand for the ceremony. Dick's father was his best man, and one of my friends, Sara, from college, was my maid of honor. Both stood at our sides.

I was wearing a knee-length blue dress, lightly decorated with fashion jewelry. Dick sported black slacks, a white dress shirt, and a handsome wine-colored tie.

It was 1:55 p.m. when the city clerk started the ceremony. Passionately, I smiled at my future husband and placed my hand in his. The ceremony started with the clerk stating the typical wording of a wedding and ended with, "Do you, Richard, take this woman, Diann, to be your lawfully wedded wife, to have and to hold, from this day forward, for better, for worse, for richer, for poorer, in sickness and in health, until death do you part?"

"I do," Dick said with a smile. My heart pounded with glee.

The clerk repeated the same words to me, and I replied, "I do," with the biggest grin.

"I now pronounce you, husband and wife."

As he spoke those words, the two o'clock hour approached, and the cuckoo clock on the flowered wallpapered wall made its strike, with the sound of "Cuckoo, cuckoo!" Is this a sign? I thought to myself.

We celebrated our nuptials directly after the ceremony with our witnesses at the same local Chinese restaurant where we had our first date. Enjoying pork fried rice, sweet and sour chicken, and Mai Tai's was quite a delight.

That evening we went our separate ways because Dick didn't have a home, as he lived at the YMCA, and I stayed in my dorm. *So romantic…*

The next day, I asked my parents to meet us at my mother's house. We informed my parents of the wedding. My mother wasn't upset at all that we were married, and my father didn't show any emotion. He just shook Dick's hand and said, "Good luck."

Three days later, I graduated from college with

my associate's degree. We planned to move to Florida the following day. For some reason, Dick wanted to move away from everyone.

If only I knew then what I know now... How many of us have said that in our lifetime! I had no idea what a healthy relationship looked like, nor was I ever taught. I was taught by example at home as to how man and wife were to be treated. When a guy started showing me affection, I gravitated toward it. Dick paid attention to me. We went out and had a good time. I fell in love quickly. Or what I thought was love. I was young and naïve. I didn't know any better. The added benefit was that he was easy on the eyes. Was that all that was important to me at the time at age nineteen? The only plan I had made with my life is I wanted to be a legal secretary. I figured I could find a law firm and work anywhere. He wanted to marry me, so of course, I said yes. It was that easy.

I was flying by the seat of my pants, entering into this marriage. I had a lot of lessons to learn in the upcoming year.

***

I was young and in love and now moving to Florida. This was quite an exciting adventure. We left early on a sunny Monday morning, with as many belongings that would fit in my car.

We made the long 1600-mile drive to Fort Lauderdale in twenty-seven hours, arriving at the beach on Tuesday afternoon. We arrived virtually broke. We could not afford an apartment, so we settled for a room at the Sans Souci Motel, on Birch Road about a block from the beach, and stayed all summer long. Fortunately for us, it was summer, which is the off-season, so rooms were at a reasonable discount, and you could pay by the week.

As our meager funds ran low, we knew we needed to find jobs. But until we did, we'd give blood, which would give us just enough to buy peanut butter and bread. We even went to pawn shops, pawning whatever we could to get some money to survive. At one point, I even pawned my high school ring. I think we only received twenty dollars, but it helped us out tremendously. This was not a lifestyle I was accustomed to, but I didn't care. I was with Dick, and to me, this was a sensational life, and that was all that mattered.

Soon, I found work as a secretary, making enough money to sustain us. Then Dick found a job selling cars, although that would not last long.

Dick would move from one job to the other. He'd get a job, and just as quickly, he'd lose it. Later, I would discover the reason. He would drink on the job, and of course, businesses do not tolerate that! So it was left up to me to bring in the "bacon" to pay for our room, food, and gas. This was not what I had expected from a loving marriage. But I thought, give it some time.

Like most couples, we argued. But ours were

becoming more and more frequent. His drinking did not help matters. He was an angry drunk. The uglier our argument got, the worse his anger raged. During one of these arguments, after being married for only two months, I screamed at him, "Dick, why do you drink so much? Can't you just lay off it?" I was angry with him and wished my marriage hadn't turned out to be such a disaster.

Dick stumbled to my side, stunningly calm, and replied, "Hon, this is so hard for me. I never told you, but this is a disease for me. I was going to AA meetings when we met. I went off the wagon when we started dating. I had been going for a year. I had lost jobs, was low on money, and ended up losing my apartment. That is why I ended up at the Y. I feel like such a failure."

I felt bad for him. *Why do I have to push him*? I was nineteen years old, newly married, and had no idea how to handle this situation. I only knew one way, and that was to coddle him. This is the worst way to help any alcoholic, but I knew of no other way.

For the next few days, things would be fine, then all hell would break loose again. I would go to work, come home at five thirty, and he would be sitting by the pool with one of the female guests staying at the hotel. I'd see this, and the hair on the back of my neck would stand up. I would be seething.

I would call to him in a stern voice, "Dick, would you come upstairs with me, please!" He rose slowly from his chair and just shook his head. I proceeded up to our room, put my keys and purse on the kitchen table. Then, SLAM, I'd hear the door shut.

"What do you want now? I was sitting there relaxing. You come home and interrupt me! What's that all about?" he said with a bitter voice.

I was incredulous. "It's bad enough you don't work, but do you have to hang out with girls and drink all day?" I could feel my stomach knot and my head want to blow up. "Instead of looking for a job to help us out financially? We will need to find a new place to live soon." I held on to the kitchen chair for support. "I come home from work, and you act as if you don't even care." I pushed the chair toward him. "Why didn't you get up, come and give me a hug and a kiss, and be happy I was home?" *Here's that feeling again of not being loved and wanted.*

"Diann, give me a break. You know I've been looking and can't find a job anywhere," he yelled across the room and started to bolt toward me.

He hadn't been looking for a job. Every few days, he'd say the same thing, just to keep me off his back, and he ignored my question about coming to me. He had been loud. I knew the vacationers by the pool got an earful.

I stood there glaring at him. I was standing next to the open jalousie windows when he charged at me. The next thing I knew, his right fist swung at my head. I turned, he missed, and instead hit the jalousie window, breaking one pane.

I froze, not knowing what to say or do. I'd never had anyone try to hit me. I started picking up the broken glass and remember cutting my hand, and it bled profusely. Dick saw me bleeding.

"Go rinse that off. I've got this," he ordered.

I wrapped my hand with a paper towel until it stopped bleeding and then put a bandage on it. It looked as though it needed stitches, but I ignored that fact because we wouldn't have been able to afford the hospital bill. We didn't speak about the incident. I changed into my jean shorts and a tank top. We each grabbed a beer and headed to the pool.

Everyone who was at the pool glanced at us because they had heard everything, but not a word was spoken. That is until Dick started up a conversation with the girl he had been sitting with earlier. Just like that, I thought to myself. *I can't believe this!*

Dick started hitting me a week after this incident. It was after another argument when I brought up his drinking one evening. He got irate. Dick was yelling at me, threw one of the table lamps across the room, punched the wall, and then punched me in the face. Of course, I blamed myself because he was drunk, and I never should have brought it up in the first place.

The residents and the manager had heard the noise and knocked on our door.

"Is everything okay in there?" asked Bob.

"Yeah…go away," Dick yelled.

"I heard a hell of a commotion. What's going on?" asked Walt.

"Diann, are you okay?" asked Bob.

"I'm okay, Bob. Thanks," I answered through the closed door.

You could hear them all walk away, mumbling to one another. In those days, no one really got involved with domestic violence or called the police.

I had my first black eye and didn't quite know what to make of it. Why was my husband hitting me? I believed he loved me. *It is my fault, and if I just don't upset him, he won't do this again.*

The next day, I was embarrassed to go anywhere someone would see me. I tried as hard as I could to hide it with my makeup. Now I had to pay for the damage for what Dick had done to the wall and the lamp.

His behavior was a common trait of his even though I tried hard not to upset him. Many things upset him. But because of his drinking, his anger was set off quickly. One time it was just a conversation he was having with one of the residents by the pool. They asked him what he did for work, and since he wasn't working, that question pissed him off. He then got up and went to our room. I followed to try to calm him down, and the fight started between us. I got shoved, hit, and items were thrown once again. I thought I was being a good wife by trying to be by my husband's side to console him. Once again, I was wrong.

The blue-and-purple bruises on my eyes and arms were beginning to become a reoccurrence that I was getting used to.

August came, and tourist season was fast approaching. That meant we would have to find another place to live. Naturally, on just my salary, we'd never make it. Unbeknownst to us, the current managers were leaving. Dick spoke to the hotel owner and managed to finagle a way for us to become managers. So, Dick saved the day, I thought sarcastically.

We officially became managers in August, managing the twenty-six-room hotel. That meant we now would move into the manager's quarters, a one-bedroom apartment. Much more room than the confines of the one-room we had been renting. On the downside, Dick still had the luxury of drinking at all times. He had little work to do. Outside of fixing a few things in the rooms occasionally, he just "relaxed" and drank. I worked the registration desk, managed the maids, and ordered supplies, basically everything else.

Now that we were together as much as we were, he could drink more, and the fights grew worse. He was using me as a punching bag regularly, and try as I could, I could not hide the black eyes he gave me. The maids noticed and eventually would ask me if I was all right. "Of course," I would reply. I could not betray my husband. Even some vacationers feared him and would complain to me about his demeanor.

Our sex life became more and more abusive, physically and verbally. He got physically rough. But the most devastating and hurtful was the verbal abuse. Specifically, he started saying to me in a sickening tone, "*Is this the way your uncle did it to you?*" This was an obvious reference to my rape. Oh, how I cried. I'd never been able to sleep those nights. I could not believe someone could be so cruel to his wife. My trust level sank lower and lower with the frequency of the words, the screaming matches, and the ever-increasing blows to the face, the grabbing of my arms, and the punches to my back.

On the days he wasn't hitting me, we did manage to have good days. Frans, the owner of the hotel, lived in Canada and would come once a month to check the facilities. We weren't allowed to leave the premises together any other times, as one of us had to be there since we were managers. This did put another strain on the marriage. When the owner was in town, we took some much-needed time off.

We went to the beach for the entire day and enjoyed the sun and the sand. I had always loved the beach for its tranquility and went with friends and oftentimes by myself while growing up. The sound of the waves and the smell of the salt air was calming for me. Even going there with Dick provided me some peacefulness and hope.

We would swim and be silly in the water together. This meant the world to me. Here, he led me to believe that our marriage was going to be okay. He was showing me he loved me by making me happy. So I thought. We were having fun, and he wasn't drunk. As we lay on our towels on the sand, we would talk of our future which gave me expectations all would be well. He was my Prince Charming once again. Until we'd go back to the hotel, and life would go on as usual.

We only managed the Sans Souci for nine months. The hotel owner had been receiving numerous complaints about Dick's behavior, so we were told we were out of a job, which also meant we were out of a place to live.

We started searching for a new place to manage, and as luck would have it, we found a condo complex a few miles up A1A in Pompano Beach. This was a much easier job, as the units were individually owned, and we only had to perform repairs when needed. We also took messages for residents and got the condos ready when the owners were returning. Piece of cake, right? Not really. He still had time for his drinking.

The jobs at the hotel and condo had one major drawback. One of us still had to always be on the premises, and this became a major issue for Dick and subsequently for me. He became suspicious any time I left the property. I would have to leave to go to the grocery store and to pick up supplies. He was too drunk to make the trip by himself. He would time me to see how long I was gone, thinking I was doing something other than what I said I was going to do. He would also make sure all my chores were done and completed 100 percent correctly, going over them with a fine-tooth comb. If he felt they were not done to his satisfaction, he would scream at me to do them over again. Countless fights occurred because of these things. Maybe, naively, I believed this would never have happened if he had not been drinking.

The arguments grew more frequent if that was possible. He was hitting me, shoving me, kicking me, throwing things at me, more and more. More bruises. More secrets. More locked doors. I was walking on eggshells, automated behavior. After all, he was thirteen years my senior. Shouldn't I obey? This is what I was taught. This is all I knew.

One night the fight was horrific. He picked me up and slammed me against the bedroom dresser, my face hitting first. This was the beginning of the end. I had reached the end of my rope.

He owned a flare gun. Although he had never pointed it at me, I was terrified he would use it. That night I took the gun, ran out the back door, and threw it into the ocean. I stood there thinking for a moment, went back to the apartment, and called 911. When the deputies arrived, I told them what had happened and that this wasn't the first time he had abused me. They could clearly see my bulging black eye and the lump on my head. But the two deputies, as incredible as it may seem, laughed about it with Dick, and then they left. *Really, that's it?* Going on the word of the wife beater instead of the beaten-up wife? Wow…Thank God laws have changed in the past years regarding domestic violence. This would never happen today.

I had enough. The next day, Dick left the house to restock his alcohol habit. I called my mother, told her what had happened, and we decided it was best I return to Maine. My brother Guy lived in an adjacent city and came to my rescue. We threw as much of my clothing as we could into his car and bolted from the apartment before Dick returned home.

We drove to my brother's house, and he said to me, "Diann, let me purchase you the airline ticket to head to Mom's. I know you don't have the money, and God knows you need to get out of here."

At the sound of those words, my heart flooded with love. I hadn't been spoken to so sweetly and lovingly in a long time. What a sweetheart my brother was. And with that, he purchased an airline ticket for me to "get out of Dodge." I could just imagine the look on Dick's face when he arrived home! Priceless!

CHAPTER 6

Life after Divorce

I WAS HEADING BACK to my mother's house. A place where my life was in turmoil in my early years, not that long ago. I didn't think my world was going to be this way at this time of my life, but there I was, heading north. I found it the only choice I had at the time. A prisoner escaping to her world. Albeit, I was fortunate I had a place to go. I didn't dare tell my father what Dick had done to me yet, and living with my brother at that time wasn't an option. I wanted to get as far away from Dick as I could.

I flew from Ft. Lauderdale to New York. Then I had to wait in LaGuardia Airport overnight, as my connecting flight to Maine had been canceled. Trying to rest, I lay on the floor with my head on my suitcase overnight. It was early the next morning I boarded the plane, with my head held low, hoping no one would question my protruding, black-and-blue left eye. I could feel the stares. I found my seat toward the end of the row. It felt good to finally be on the plane. In an hour, I would arrive at the Portland Jetport.

My smiling mother greeted me with a hug. No words were spoken. That's all I needed at the time. It meant the world to me.

The party world continued. Of course, being at Mom's house, what else is there going to be? I was still in shock after what had just gone on in my life with my husband, the philanderer, an abusive drunk.

Mom wanted to take me out the same night I arrived to "celebrate" the fact that I left my husband.

"Mom, I don't feel like going out tonight. Plus, look at my face. Not something I want people to see. Let's stop at Grampie's house so I can get a hug from him, then call it a night."

Mom wouldn't hear of it.

"No, Diann. You need a few drinks to calm down. You've gone through so much. Trust me, you'll feel better. We'll go to Grampie's in a few days."

So that was that. I was twenty years old and still felt as though I had to listen to my mother and go along with her. As little self-esteem I had left after my rape, I had lost the rest of it while being married to Dick. Once again, I was numb.

Mom and I went out to the Holiday Inn that night and met two guys, Scott and Alex. We partied until closing time. We took them both home at the end of the evening and continued to party. I was vulnerable, lonely, and enjoyed the attention. I drank too much and passed out in my bed with Scott.

I put things in motion a few days later and filed for divorce. Dick asked if we could try again. My response was a flat, "NO."

A month later, I wasn't feeling well. I chalked it up to all that had been going on and my nerves. So I let it be. A week later, I realized why I hadn't been feeling well. I was late. I purchased a home pregnancy test, and it revealed I was pregnant.

I was elated. I didn't press the issue for Scott to be responsible for the baby. I wanted to take care of my baby on my own. I was in no position to be in another relationship at that time of my life.

Two months later, Dick and I met in court. Quick and simple. Dick and I signed the divorce papers. Done deal. I was free!

When I was four months pregnant, I moved back to Florida to get away from all the partying that was happening in my mother's home. I couldn't be a part of it. I was comfortable living in the Ft. Lauderdale area and knew my way around. I wanted a place of my own and to get on my own two feet. I was happy I was going to have a baby.

My father helped me out financially with a car, an apartment, and getting settled in. I had saved some money with my job, but not enough to move 1600 miles and get my own place.

After getting settled into my apartment, my father came to visit me. He stated I should give my baby up for adoption.

"Diann, there is an agency on University Drive next to the mall, and I suggest you make an appointment."

Could I do this to my baby? Could I not handle raising a child? How could my father not believe in me? Nope, not going to do it. I let my father believe I was going to go through with his suggestion of giving my baby away. I didn't want to hear anything coming from him.

Determined to prove him wrong, I held my head high and conquered each day as it came. I found strength and courage as the new life grew inside. I had reason to persevere. It was time for me to take charge of my life, and now, my child's as well.

Mom suggested she move to Florida and live with me. I was hesitant at first, but she made a persuasive case. I thought sharing expenses might be good, and she could help with babysitting. So, Mom moved in when I was eight months along.

We got along pretty well. Obviously, she wasn't taking me out partying, and she didn't go anywhere because she knew no one in the area. However, she continued to drink heavily, and by dinnertime, she'd be a tad tipsy. But I could handle that; after all, I was used to it.

The day finally arrived, June 5, 1986, the day my son Kurt came into the world. My newborn son arrived in the late morning. What a bundle of joy this nine-pound twelve-ounce, blond-haired, blue-eyed son was to me. The nurse handed him to me, and my face lit up like a Christmas tree. My heart pulsated as if it were about to come out of my chest. He is mine. All mine. My heart was full.

Life was different. I finally knew what love was. As a mother, my world was complete. Each breath I took, I took for Kurt. I cherished every moment with him.

What I still didn't know at the time was what a healthy relationship looked like, but I kept promising my son and myself that I would do everything in my power to raise him the best way I could. I was learning day to day.

***

It was August, and with Kurt about six weeks old, it was time to go back to work. I went to work at a restaurant named "Wags." It was like a Denny's, on South Federal Highway in Fort Lauderdale. Working at a restaurant was not my first pick, but it was close to where I was living, and since I'd just had Kurt, I wanted the flexibility of the hours.

It was here at Wag's where I believed in love at first sight.

It was August 16, a Saturday night, about seven, and sitting in a rear booth in my section were two Fort Lauderdale police officers. Mario was in plain clothes; his belt prominently displayed his badge. I had met Mario before during one of his evening breaks with his partner.

I walked to their booth and handed them menus. Mario introduced me to the officer sitting across from him.

"Diann, this is my brother, Joe." Oh, I could feel the butterflies in my stomach. Joe had dark hair with a mustache with brown eyes. When he glanced at me, my heart pounded.

I couldn't believe how I was feeling. I guess maybe I was a sucker for a man in uniform, but it wasn't just that. There was something wonderful about the way he spoke to me. I left and returned a few minutes later with their coffee and took their orders. Once placing their order on their table, I repeatedly returned to be sure they were well taken care of. I think they were the two best-served customers that night.

I continued to think about Joe and started asking the other servers about him. Only a few knew of him, as they told me he worked the midnight shift for the police department. *Hmm…now that means I need to work the midnight shift if I want to see him again.*

It was another week before I saw Joe again. He arrived at four in the morning to take his break along with other officers.

"Hello there. I thought you worked the evening shift," he said with that gorgeous smile.

"I was, but I changed it." I didn't want him knowing I changed my shift just for him. I noticed on the faces of the other officers at the table they were aware of the electricity between us. As I left the table, I could hear the other officers making comments to him.

"Oh, that server has a thing for you, Joe. Did you see how her eyes were beaming at you?" Sgt. Don Wallace said with a smile.

These nights became a regular occurrence throughout the following weeks. Each morning around 4:00 a.m., I always grew anxious for the men in uniforms to arrive.

A few mornings, Joe came by the restaurant alone. During these times, it gave us a chance to talk alone, away from his buddies. By this time, my manager and the rest of the crew could see my growing excitement and expectations with him. I would take my breaks when he came and would sit and talk with him.

I only lived a block from the restaurant, so each morning, I would walk home. This area was a mix of apartments and businesses along South Federal Highway. It wasn't the best of neighborhoods. But it was all I could afford, so it was home.

One morning as I was walking home from work, a brown police car came rolling up beside me as I reached my apartment complex. It startled me at first, then I saw who was driving. I had no idea he even knew where I lived, but it felt good to know that he did. He had brought me Dunkin' Donuts coffee and started making small talk. Never in my life had I had coffee, but I would not deny him!

"You scared me driving up like that! How did you know where I lived?"

He got out of his car and sat on the trunk. He told me, "I was patrolling one day and saw you walking home. I assumed you lived here. I kept an eye out to make sure you made it home safely. It's not safe for a young mother to be walking home alone in this area."

Over the next few weeks, I'd see Joe at work, and most mornings, he'd meet me outside my apartment for coffee. We were still getting to know each other.

One morning after work, he brought coffee, and I said to Joe, "Let's go into my apartment."

Joe sat down in my living room. I had a brown, orange, and black couch. I couldn't stand the colors, but at least it was comfortable. I had purchased all my furniture at Goodwill, but I had always made sure it was sturdy and clean. "Come sit beside me," Joe said as he sat with his coffee.

I gingerly sat next to him. I was rather anxious. I couldn't believe Joe was in my house. And now here I was, sitting down next to him.

"Now that we have some alone time, let's talk. Let's really get to know one another. You already know some of my past. I want to know all about you, Diann." I felt myself sink into the cushion of the couch.

When I heard these words, I became worrisome.

What would I tell him? I honestly didn't want him to know *all* about me. I didn't want him to know about my past. I felt as though I was used goods, and if he knew about me, he wouldn't want to have anything to do with me. I liked him and didn't want to screw this up.

"Honestly, Joe, I don't know where to start. Okay, I was born in Massachusetts but grew up in Maine." I stopped with those words and hesitated. Moments passed by.

"Yes…what else?" Joe chuckled. I felt my face go from relaxed to ruddy, and Joe noticed it too. "What's wrong?"

My gut tightened right into my belly button, and I became defensive. "Okay. I'll be honest with you. There are things in my past I'd rather you didn't know. There are things I'm quite ashamed of." A wave of depression washed over me. "I'm afraid you won't want to be with me if you know of them." There, now I'd said it. Through the dim, it made me feel good that I was honest with him.

"Diann. Please." Joe reached for my hand, and I pulled away. "Don't worry about your past. That is your past. It's made you who you are today. I will not judge you. I think you are a wonderful person."

I felt myself melt. Yet deep inside, all I wanted to do was run.

"You are sweet, obviously honest, you are a passionate mother, and I am very interested in you.

Please don't be afraid to mention anything to me. You will not scare me away."

With those words, I informed him of my childhood, marriage, and divorce. He sat there and listened to me intently. He didn't raise an eye once. Hmm, I thought. I didn't scare him!

"Now it's your turn, Joe. I want you to tell me about you. What was your childhood like, where did you go to school, and what did you do after school? How did you get into police work?" I asked as I wanted to get the attention away from the details of my life. I didn't want him asking me questions right now.

"As you know, I was born in Key West and raised near Miami. I already told you about some of my life, so here's the rest of the story." Joe pulled up from the couch and folded his arms in front of him.

As he proceeded to fill me in on the history of his life to date, I sat in amazement of this man and thought I could fall in love with him.

"…and I'm really glad I met you last month," he said with an enormous grin.

An odd feeling of relief filled me, and my heart melted. Did I hear what I thought I heard? I felt the magnetism immediately.

We truly enjoyed one another. As time went on, we would go out to dinner, clubs, and relaxed in my apartment, enjoying one another's company.

I wasn't stressed. Joe wasn't like Dick at all. He

made me feel comfortable. He made me feel safe. He respected me. I felt free to talk to him about Dick and Sal, and that helped me immensely, as I didn't have any other support system. It didn't take long for me to get everything off my chest. We could communicate well, and to me, that was important. The problem I had from the abuse was, I was extremely jealous. I brought that baggage with me into this relationship because of Dick's behaviors.

But after a year and a half, we weren't ready to get married. I had reached my limit and was impatient and immature, and I broke up with him. I would not wait any longer. It truly broke my heart, but I thought this was the best thing for me at the time. So we parted.

Six months later, my son and I moved into a small two-bedroom apartment in a city close by. By this time, Mom had found her own apartment and continued to live in Fort Lauderdale. She visited often, but it was wonderful to have a place of my own.

I started working at a real estate development company as an executive assistant and doing well for myself. As a single mother, I felt well accomplished. I did not know what my father was so worried about.

Being a working single mom was rewarding yet daunting at the same time. I loved my son with all of my heart, but occasionally I needed a break from it all. I wanted to continue with my social life. Go to work, raise my child, pay my bills, and go out dancing. Fortunately, Mom was always willing to babysit. I demanded she did not drink in my house while being with my son. Although years later, that went out the window.

One night, I bumped into Joe at a club. I walked over to his table, and we talked for a few minutes. He never asked me to dance, so I went back to my area by the dance floor. It hurt me he didn't want to spend any time with me, but I had to accept it.

One specific night I remember was when I met David. You couldn't miss him! He was tall, had dark hair, and extremely handsome with a great build. It was obvious he took great care of himself. He was with his friend Rick. David approached me and asked me to dance, and I replied, "I'd love to!" I was always eager to respond to someone who was giving me attention. We danced to a few songs, and then he asked me to come back to his table to join his friend Rick. We had the basic small talk and found out David was self-employed and a single dad with custody of his children. There weren't many fathers that had custody of their children, and that impressed me.

David and I dated for three to four months. He was sweet. We'd go out to dinner, he'd cook me dinner at his place, or we would go to the movies. One day, my mom and David were both at my apartment, and Mom hit on David. I was disgusted and embarrassed for David. David just shrugged it off.

When Kurt was sick and couldn't go to daycare, David helped by babysitting. I thought this was nice of him since I had to go to work. David was a kind soul and would do anything for me. I felt a lot for David, but it wasn't love.

I was happy in our relationship but felt too close to him, so I started pushing him away. I didn't want a commitment. Our relationship fizzled out, and I felt bad. I did like David. I had no idea where to place my feelings for him.

CHAPTER 7

Jim

THERE WAS A FUN-FILLED nightclub on North Federal Highway in Fort Lauderdale. Flashing strobe lights and a large crowd full of laughter. It was 1989. My friend, Darrah, whom I had met at Kurt's daycare the previous year, and I both had a manicure earlier in the day. Our nails looked fabulous. Both painted pink, and mine matched my blouse that evening.

We were having such a great time dancing the night away when suddenly I felt a tap on my brightly colored shoulder. "Would you care to dance?" he asked coyly.

"Sure." *Why not?*

We danced the rest of the evening together. We had a great time. Jim had a great sense of humor, and even my friend Darrah could tell he was trying to get me to like him. He lacked in the looks department, but his personality made up for it. He worked hard for me to like him by telling us jokes, offering to buy us drinks, and keeping us company. He eventually got my phone number.

"So, Diann, would you like to get together sometime and have dinner?"

I thought to myself for a moment and answered, "Yes, that would be fine." I had a great time that evening, and why not go out with someone who helped make my night entertaining.

We dated, spent many nights on the phone discussing our lives, our likes, and dislikes. Our relationship seemed to blossom.

I was beginning to like this guy. He wasn't handsome. He was on the short side, and he was balding. I suppose what attracted me to him was his demeanor. He treated me as if I were special to him, which is exactly what I'd always wanted in my life. He was attentive, spoiled me with gifts, and best of all, always wanted to be with me.

He was the vice president of a local business and was involved in the community. I felt I landed myself a professional man, which would make my father happy. I still wanted to impress my father.

About three months into our relationship, certain things should have "clicked" in my brain. Unfortunately, they didn't. My antennas eventually went up, but not far enough for my brain to say, "Stop, this guy is a freak!" I didn't know about red flags. They didn't come naturally to me.

One night while heading out to a club with Jim,

I was freshening my mascara using the visor mirror in his car. He slammed on the brakes, on purpose. When he did this, the mascara wand nearly pushed into my eye. I shot him a look, silently telling him I was both angry and thought he was nuts, but he counteracted with an expression that shut me up.

In hindsight, I should have realized that was pretty absurd and not the type of guy I should have been dating. I learned later this was a part of the "grooming" process, and he was trying to see how far he could push me and what I would say or not say to him. How assertive was I? I said nothing. So obviously not assertive at all.

The dating continued, and the relationship evolved. After only six months, we moved in together. With Kurt in tow, we moved in with Jim along with his fourteen-year-old daughter.

All went well for a few months. Then we took the kids out to breakfast one morning. We were having a conversation that was leading up to an argument.

"Let's just stop talking. It's not worth it," I said. He then reached across the table and slapped me across the face. Right there in public, in front of the children! I was speechless. I know what I would do today if that happened, take my kid and leave. However, I was twenty-four at the time and had no earthly idea what to do. No one spoke throughout the rest of the meal. I allowed that to happen. I just sat back and kept quiet. Once we all finished our meals, we left, and life went on.

Jim and I went out another night, and he caused another incident while he was driving. We were bantering in the car. He ended up getting irate. He leaned over me, opened my car door, and pushed me out onto Oakland Park Blvd. A four-lane divided roadway with a 35-mph speed limit and always busy with traffic. Thankfully, he wasn't driving this fast, and I wasn't seriously injured. There was a gas station nearby which I ran to, after getting quickly to my feet.

I ran into the station, out of breath and scared to death, and I told the clerk what had happened.

"Oh, I saw it all happen," the clerk replied with a worried look.

"Is there a place I can hide?" I asked quickly as my body shook with shock from fear. He let me hide in the storage area. A few minutes later, Jim came and asked the clerk where I went, as he had seen me run into the station. The clerk lied, telling him he had no idea what he was talking about. Eventually, Jim left, and the clerk called 911 for me. Once the police arrived, I filed a report. I had a great eyewitness.

"Ma'am, do you have a safe place to go tonight?" the officer asked.

"Yes, I'll call my mother. My son is with her now. I'll spend the night with her. Thank you, officer, for all your help. I appreciate it."

I called my mother and asked her to pick me up. I stayed the night at her apartment. I went back to my apartment with Jim the next day, *like a fool.* Jim was apologetic. He told me how sorry he was and that he would never do such a thing again. He took all the blame. I forgave him. I never followed up with the police.

One night, we were at a nightclub, and Mackenzie Phillips was performing that evening. We were dancing and having fun when suddenly he got mad about a guy looking at me, and he hauled off and punched me right in the face. Jim was extremely jealous and would get upset with me if other guys looked at me. As people in the club looked on, I got so pissed at him I left. I was much younger, fourteen years younger, than Jim. I can only imagine people asking themselves why we were together.

That night after I left him at the club, I started walking home, which was a three-mile hike, but I didn't care. A police officer stopped me while walking along the road and asked, "Miss, are you okay?" I assured him I would be fine, and he drove off. When I arrived home, Jim was already there.

Jim started yelling at me. Telling me it wasn't right that I left him at the club and that others looked at me the way they were. I explained to him it wasn't my fault they looked at me. He didn't want to hear it and kicked me and pushed me to the floor. Thankfully, he left the house, and I went to bed.

While cooking dinner, another big fight ensued, and I lost again. I was cooking his favorite meal in the wok. I was proud to be able to serve it to him. As he watched me cook, he noticed I wasn't adding the right ingredients.

He yelled, "You are so stupid! You can't do it like that! You should know better."

I moved over and said in a calm tone, "You can finish cooking the meal."

He didn't like that response, so he shoved me aside and punched me in the face. It seemed so easy for him to do this. Another black eye to add to all the others, and I didn't leave. But at the time, and still being young, I guess I felt obligated to him. I loved him. He always treated me well when he was having good days, and I always felt he would change.

Another fight developed when we got home from a club. He stormed up the stairs to the bedroom. As fast as he went up, right back down, he came. I was in the kitchen, trying to stay away from him. Cornered and scared, I tried to scoot around him to run up the stairs, but that upset him even more. He grabbed me, turned me around, and BOOM with his fist straight to my face. I stumbled to the stairs, managed to get to my feet, and ran up straight into our bedroom.

His worried daughter came into my bedroom moments later, asking, "Why do you stay with him?"

My response, "Because I love him." It was obvious even to a fifteen-year-old, this was not the right way to live your life.

Manipulation and broken promises were all a part

of my life in the following months. Oh, yes, and more bruises. Why was I continuing to put up with this? Every time he gave me another black-and-blue, he then became Prince Charming, which again gave me hope. He would beg for my forgiveness, declaring his love for me, promising me it was the last time. I was hoping things would change. I loved him and believed he would stop. I always felt he deserved another chance.

After yet another black eye, it was finally time to leave. I had enough. I found a cute two-bedroom apartment on the first floor for my son and me. Thankfully, I was working full time and could be financially independent. Unfortunately, it was only two miles down the road from where Jim and I had been living. I soon learned living this close to Jim was not the best decision for starting a new life.

Jim, the abuser, now became the stalker. One night I was at the Holiday Inn, close to my former home with Jim. It was around the corner from my new apartment. I was out with my friend Darrah. We were having a good time dancing until we saw Jim outside. I was furious. Thankfully, David's friend Rick was there, and I went and talked to him.

"Rick, can you please call David to come here? My ex is outside, and that tells me only trouble is about to happen."

"Of course, Diann. I'll dial him right now," Rick responded.

David only lived a few blocks away and got there in ten minutes flat. He knew about Jim and me and our bad living situation, as I had talked to him over the phone since our breakup. He had also seen Jim in the past when he and I both were at the Holiday Inn, and this was not the first occurrence of Jim stalking me when I went out.

"Diann, what's going on?" David said ever so affectionately after he arrived.

"Didn't you see Jim outside?"

"I just did. He's just standing there like an idiot."

"Yes. He's stalking me again. I'm sure he's just waiting for me to leave so he can see where I go," I replied.

"Well, we can start with this. See how he is looking in? Want to make this interesting?"

"Sure, what do you have in mind?" I asked him curiously.

"Act as if we are dating again. I'll put my arm around you. Maybe this will tell him you are with someone, and he'll leave you alone," David said with confidence.

"I am game for anything. I just want him to leave me alone."

So, for the next two hours, David and I acted as if we were an item. Jim eventually walked into the club. He stood far enough away from us, not to cause a scene, but close enough to be within good staring distance. This was making me nervous, and I was shaking. I couldn't stand it anymore.

"David, I just have to go. I can't handle this. Can you come to my apartment?"

"Let's go, Diann. Anything you want. Just don't look at him when we leave."

We proceeded out of the Holiday Inn, and I got in my car, and David followed me. We arrived at my apartment in five minutes. It wasn't fifteen minutes later when there was a knock on the door. Out of the corner of my eye, I saw something out the window. I went and looked, and I could see Jim walking away. *DAMN IT.*

Peeping through the windows of my apartment and following me frequently was what I was dealing with at the time. I would simply be going to the grocery store, and all of a sudden, I would look into my rearview mirror, and there he was, right behind me. I would weave in and out of cars along the route, and then he'd be gone in a flash. He just wanted to make himself known. My anxiety level reached a new height. When I was alone in my home with my son, I had no idea what Jim was going to do next. He would leave gifts at my door, ring the doorbell at all hours, and act like the best escape artist in town.

My next move was getting a restraining order. I was granted a one-year protection order. This aggravated him more. Even with the restraining order, he stalked me at work. He would sit in his car in the parking lot at my office and waited for me to come out at lunchtime or after work. He'd try to talk me into moving back into his home. I was scared out of my mind and thought he would try to kill me at this point. You never knew what Jim was going to do next. After all the abuse I endured, my mind started playing tricks on me. My antennae were always heightened.

Every time I saw him stalking me, I'd call the police. Since I had the restraining order, the police would come, but by the time they got to my house or work, Jim would be gone. "Sorry, ma'am, but we couldn't find him."

"So, what do I do the next time he is near me? He is getting away with it every time," I said in a terrified voice.

"Keep calling us. We will get him eventually." As he replied to me, I felt hopeless. I'd been calling the police each time Jim was near us, but each time he would be gone before the police arrived.

I called David and told him what I had been going through that past month. He told me he was going to put a stop to this himself. One evening, David hid in the bushes outside my window at home and waited for Jim. It didn't take an hour for Jim to arrive. When Jim's legs got close enough to the bush where David was hiding, David grabbed his legs and took him to the ground. Now the fight was on.

Unfortunately, during the fight, Jim tore David's right shoulder ACL. As for Jim, he got away yet again. I am ever so grateful for David helping me every time.

He was such a wonderful friend, and I needed him. There aren't many men out in this world who would come to a woman's rescue during such a time.

Jim knew me pretty well and knew the right buttons to push to get his way with me. A few months later, Jim sent his daughter to talk to me. He knew I couldn't send her away. Rachel and I had been close for the time she lived with us, and my heart was always with her.

Rachel came to me and told me that her dad was sorry he had hurt me and been following me. She said he loved me and wanted me to move back into the apartment with them. She told me she missed me and could use me back in the house as a friend. My heart melted with her words. I missed her too.

I was at a crossroads. I knew what Jim did was wrong, but I wanted to be with him. I felt as though he had a problem, but he loved me, so he would change. As long as I didn't upset him, he wouldn't hurt me. I would just be ever so careful not to give him any reason to get him mad.

A few months went by, and he had stopped stalking me. He was going to counseling and taking Prozac. I thought, what could go wrong? I finally gave in to him. I had faith things would change this time. I moved back in with Jim. Within two weeks, he proposed marriage, and I accepted.

CHAPTER 8

Child Abuse

SINCE WE HADN'T SPOKEN in a few years, I reached out to my father to ask him to be a part of my wedding. Every girl wants this, right?

I dialed the number in my blue phone book and waited patiently for an answer on the other end. "Hello?" As I heard the familiar voice of my father, I almost cried. I missed my father and still yearned for his love. And his acceptance.

"Hi, Dad. I know we haven't spoken in a while, but I wanted to know if we could get together. I have some news I want to discuss with you. Could we set something up?"

I could hear the hesitation in my father's voice, but he eventually replied, "Sure. How about next Sunday?" he asked.

"That works," I answered.

"Okay, how about we meet at the steakhouse in Lauderhill at five thirty?"

"Sounds good to me. Thanks, Dad. See you then."

That Sunday night, my father and I met for dinner. Kurt stayed home with Jim and his daughter.

Dinner went surprisingly well. We hadn't been in touch since shortly after Kurt had been born. Kurt was to turn five in a month. My father and I talked, trying to get to know one another again. I told him of my upcoming nuptials and asked him if he would walk me down the aisle. When we parted that evening, he didn't give me an answer.

When I returned home, Jim greeted me at the garage, which he never did. He had a strange look on his face. It made me feel eerie just looking at him. "Where's Kurt?" I asked hesitantly.

"He's in bed," Jim responded. The air felt thick and heavy as if something was wrong. I went to check on my son.

I found Kurt lying in his bed, staring at the ceiling, awake. I went in and asked him if he was okay. He said, "Daddy spanked me."

"He spanked you?" I said in horror, as I could see tears welling up in my little boy's eyes. "Where?"

Kurt pouted his lips and said, "On my butt, Mommy." His words were sullen and dejected.

Kurt called Jim daddy, even though Jim and I were not married, and he wasn't his birth father, Kurt felt Jim was daddy to him. Just hearing how he said those words and the look on his face, I knew something was dreadfully wrong. I turned him over and pulled down his pants to look at his bottom.

Still, to this day, I have seen nothing like Kurt's bottom that night. He had blood on his bottom; it was all black and blue and scraped up. His face looked as if he had seen a ghost. In retrospect, I think he was in shock.

I asked him if he was in pain, and he answered he was sore. I cleaned him up, hugged him and told him I loved him, and he was safe now. I didn't know what else to say. I sat with him for a good while, then I told him good night after giving him hugs and lots of kisses. I walked out of his bedroom and pretended nothing was wrong as I went into my bedroom. I remember thinking if I said anything to Jim, he would hurt or kill us both.

I went to bed and lay awake all night with one foot touching the floor. It seemed like forever until Jim went to work the following morning. Jim said nothing to me and acted as if he had done nothing wrong. Jim's daughter went to school, and then Kurt woke up, and I got him ready for the day.

Over a bowl of cereal, I asked Kurt again what had happened the night before.

"Daddy spanked me because I pooped in my pants." He cried and said, "Daddy took me into the bathroom, pulled down my pants, and spanked really hard with my toy ninja sword. He pushed my head under the water."

"You did nothing wrong, hon. You shouldn't have been punished for that. I want to ask you something, Kurt. After you finish your cereal, I'd like to take you for a short drive. I'd like to go to the police station. I'd like you to tell a police officer what happened last night, okay? Would you be willing to do that?"

"Okay. I will," Kurt said as he sat up in his chair. He almost sat proudly while saying those words. As if he knew that was the right thing to do.

He finished his cereal, and we drove five minutes to the police station. Officers took photographs of my son's injuries and interviewed both of us separately. Detective Mangini came out after speaking with my son and informed me I was lucky they weren't investigating a homicide case.

My heart dropped.

He told me what my son had told them, which was more detail than what Kurt had informed me the night before. The man that I "loved" took off my son's clothing, placed him in the bathtub, spanked him, held his head underwater, put a brown towel around his neck, held him up in the air by the neck with the towel, kneed him in the stomach, beat him on the buttocks with the plastic toy sword, and held him under the water again.

With these words, I shivered and wanted to cry. I was crying on the inside but needed to stay strong for Kurt, now that he was on my lap. I was in disbelief. I was in shock. I couldn't believe Jim would do this to my son. I was hurting for my child and felt horrible he had gone through this torment. I hugged Kurt tighter.

Is this my fault too? If I didn't leave him alone last night with Jim, this never would have happened. Why did I leave him to meet with my father? This IS my fault. If I had never gone back to live with Jim after all the beatings, this wouldn't have happened. What have I done?

It was at that point the detectives wanted to bring Kurt and me to our house. Jim was at work, so they wanted Kurt to describe everything that went on in the house to them without Jim there.

Kurt showed the detectives his bedroom and how he was led to the bathroom. He then brought them to the laundry room and removed the brown towel from the dryer Jim had used to hang him up by the neck. I was proud of Kurt. He was doing such a magnificent job and staying strong.

At that point, the phone rang. Detective Mangini told me if it was Jim to keep him on the line. He wanted to listen on the other line to get some information. He also wanted me to try to get him to come home so they could arrest him.

"Hello?" I said, trying to stay calm.

"What are you doing home? I called work. You weren't there, and Kurt wasn't at daycare. What the hell have you been up to all day?" Jim snuffed through the line.

"Um. Kurt was sick, so I stayed home with him. Why don't you come home early so you can help take care of him with me?"

"I'm not buying that. Something is up," he snarled. It was with those words I got extremely upset.

"Yes, something is up, Jim. You did unbelievable things to Kurt last night. He is in pain. What is your problem? How could you do this to him? He didn't deserve any of this." After I said those words, he had hung up the phone. The police weren't able to catch him to admit his wrongdoings.

The police asked me if I had a safe place to stay until Jim was arrested. I informed them I would stay at the Holiday Inn until they let me know they arrested him. Then I'd worry about where to live after that.

I grabbed enough clothing for Kurt and myself to last a few days, then left to go to the Holiday Inn. I was still in shock with disbelief all this was happening. All the while keeping Kurt close to me.

It was two days later I received the infamous phone call from Detective Mangini that Jim had been arrested at work! They charged him with Aggravated Battery, two charges of Child Abuse, two charges of Aggravated Child Abuse; Willfully tortures a child, and Neglects child, or deprives of necessities, causing physical or mental injury.

He went to jail but was bonded out by evening. I stayed another few nights at the hotel until I could think of somewhere to live.

That next day, I went to the house to grab the rest of my belongings while Jim was at work. I had the police at the house to accompany me for my safety. There were TV reporters in my driveway. People were in shock that Jim would do such a thing because he was prominent in the community. People don't realize how others act behind closed doors.

My angel and I then moved. We stayed at an apartment within a hotel on the beach. Since we had to move in a hurry, this was our best bet. We didn't have to put a deposit down, like a typical apartment. I knew we would not be staying there long; plus, Kurt and I loved the ocean. This would be a nice place to relax and try to gather my thoughts. The sound of the ocean waves and the smell of the salt air always had a way of relaxing me, and Kurt loved to play in the sand.

A month after the horrid experience, I was driving along Alligator Alley to visit my father. My son was in the back in his car seat singing along to Disney songs.

After the two-hour drive, we pulled into my father's driveway and were greeted by the gang of three; my father, stepmother, and "sister." My dad and stepmother, who is eight years older than me, adopted a baby from another country a year after Kurt was born. Joy was adorable. It felt kind of odd, my father having had a child younger than my son. But it was Dad's life, and I accepted the situation.

While Kurt and my sister played with their toys

in the living room, Dad, Marta, and I talked in the kitchen. We didn't want the kids to hear us. I explained the abuse to them in detail.

"Dad, never in my wildest dreams did I think Jim would do this to Kurt. He abused me often, but I never thought he would actually hurt him."

"Diann, it is not surprising a man who hurts a woman would eventually target her child. What were you thinking by staying with this man?" There it was. The guilt. The blame. As if that was what I needed to hear.

"Dad, I loved Jim and thought he would stop hurting me. So no, I never thought he would hurt Kurt. I don't appreciate you making me feel worse about this situation than I already do." I surprised myself with my words to my father.

I reiterated that Jim got arrested and informed him of his charges. I spoke to my father about my desire to have Kurt receive counseling.

"I don't think you and Kurt need counseling," Dad responded.

With those words, my heart dropped. I didn't question my father because I learned you don't question him, and I was already upset with his earlier words. Why didn't my father think we needed counseling? We had gone through a horrible tragedy, and he didn't feel we needed counseling? I ignored his comment.

We continued with small talk at that point, then

Dad suddenly said to me, "Diann, we have forgiven Jim for what he has done to Kurt. The Bible says you need to forgive, and this is what we have done. This is something you need to do, as well."

CHAPTER 9

Life After Abuse

THE DAYS FOLLOWED CONSISTED of meetings with Child Protective Services (CPS), the Broward County State Attorney's Office (SAO), and others involved in preparations for court proceedings. I had hoped for some time to relax and get my head on straight, but with all these meetings, I got more stressed out. But all were necessary.

These meetings seemed to take forever, but the information we talked about was extremely important. CPS was asking about Kurt, how he was doing, are his injuries healing well, does he speak about the incident, and what they could do to assist us. I never asked for any support. I never felt the need.

The SAO explained the process that was now in motion. First, Jim had been arrested and had bonded out of jail almost immediately. Next would come a Probable Cause hearing, a hearing to establish that a crime had been committed, and the arrested, Jim, was the person who had committed the crime. Then would come Discovery; this is when the prosecution and the defense exchange all their evidence. It is supposed to lead to more plea agreements. The next to the last step were depositions. Finally, after all that, would come the trial or a plea hearing if Jim pleaded guilty.

The worst part of this process was how long it could take. The SAO told me it could be as quick as six months, or it could drag on for a couple of years. It all depended on the defense attorney and the tactics they chose to use.

By the time these meetings would end, my head would spin. I was spent.

I called Joe and told him what Jim had done to Kurt and the resulting arrest. I also told him about Jim abusing me and how I felt foolish for having stayed with him, but I felt so much more pain for what Jim had done to Kurt. He visited us a few times while we were staying at the beach. It was fabulous to have another support system and know someone cared.

The first knock on the door when Joe visited was exhilarating. When he came into the room and our eyes locked, it was as if time had stood still. Our love hadn't waned at all. I obviously did not mention my feelings to him; I was going through such turmoil. But I definitely felt it.

"Diann, I am so sorry for what has happened to you two."

"Thanks, Joe. Please sit down." Joe sat down on the chair next to me. And then I got my son's attention.

"Kurt, this is Joe. You probably don't remember him, but he used to know you when you were a baby!"

Kurt went up to Joe and shook his hand. Since Joe was in uniform, I could see that it actually made Kurt feel at ease. Kurt had a lot of respect for police officers since they helped him during this terrible time.

Joe and I talked for an hour that evening. We made small talk and tried not to talk about Jim because Kurt was in the room playing with his toys and didn't want him reliving the nightmare.

Even after we moved and after his arrest, Jim continued to stalk us. I'd be driving to the grocery store or to work, and somehow, he'd find me. I'd see him in my rearview mirror. My stomach churned. How in the world did he find me? Was he driving all around the area? Was he that desperate to intimidate me?

So after being abused, harassed, and continuously looking over my shoulder, we needed to move again. I had had enough of this town and the ghosts within. We planned to move 1600 miles away to the town in Maine where I grew up. *Here I go again.*

We needed stability and peace in our lives. But most importantly, I never wanted Jim to find us again.

***

Packing boxes and throwing memories away, it was time to get away from all this mess. But first, there was something I had to do. Someone I had to say goodbye to.

One evening, Joe was working a police detail on Davie Blvd., patrolling a church and parking lot. Unfortunately, churches and their parking areas were not immune from crimes, so churches hired off-duty police officers for security. Since he was alone at this detail, it gave us plenty of time to ourselves. Kurt stayed with my friend Darrah.

It was time to say goodbye before the big move. I wasn't ready to do this. I didn't want to say goodbye to him. There was no way I could leave and not see his face or kiss those lips goodbye. This pain was worse than the black-and-blues I had succumbed to with Dick or Jim. Tears flowed from the two of us like waterworks. There was no doubt in my mind about the love between us. But I had to leave. No question. Kurt's and my safety were priority number one. Joe agreed. He never once tried to convince me to stay. He understood the circumstances. Joe wanted the best for Kurt and me. We talked, cried, laughed for hours that night before the dreadful time came when we had to part.

Joe said with tears, "If only we had married, none of this would have happened to you and Kurt."

"Oh, hon. Please do not blame yourself. Sure, that would have been great. But this is not your fault.

Please do not think that." I responded with my tears. We hugged once again, longing for one another, yet knowing this was the end.

How was I going to get in my car and drive away? It was as if trying to pull magnets apart. It was nearly impossible to walk away. I could barely see through the tears as I drove off from the parking lot. Watching Joe wave to me warmed my heart, yet it hurt.

The next day, boxes were loaded into the moving van that would meet us at our new apartment in a few days. Kurt and I started our journey to our new home in New England. We drove to Sanford, Florida, where we boarded the Amtrak Auto Train. This was an exciting adventure for my five-year-old, as he had never been on a train before. He deserved some fun in his life, and I was happy to provide.

"Okay, sweetheart, let's go find our seats." Kurt's face was beaming with excitement as we walked through the bright and airy train carriage. We found our seats and sat down.

"Mom, this is really cool. We have a huge window to look out the whole ride!"

We got comfortable, and Kurt took out a few books and a toy car from his backpack. He settled down rather quickly, much to my surprise. The train traveled up the Eastern Seaboard, finally arriving outside Washington, D.C. the following morning. They unloaded our car off the train, and we then started traveling to Maine. We arrived at our new apartment that evening. Another exciting adventure.

Just the two of us. My angel and me! Kurt seemed more at ease, knowing Jim could not peek in our windows, follow us around town or bother us anymore. That meant the world to both of us, for sure. We found a safe place at last.

***

It's now mid-July and our day in court was fast approaching. There were several phone conversations with the State Attorney's Office.

I received a call from the assistant state attorney one Monday. "Diann, I'm calling to explain to you about the court date in September, and the trial is scheduled for nine a.m. Also, Kurt will have to testify at the trial. The judge ruled that he could not provide his testimony through closed-circuit TV or video."

"I'm furious with the judge for that decision, but I will get Kurt ready for the trial."

I dreaded having to do this to Kurt, but there was no other way. If I wanted Jim to pay for what he'd done to Kurt, then Kurt had to testify. I had to prepare him for that fateful day when he would have to face Jim in court.

I thought about what I could do to get Kurt ready. Then I had an idea. I arranged our living room to look like a courtroom. I used our beige living room couch and chair along with the four dark wooden chairs from the dining room set. I showed Kurt where everyone would sit, but most importantly, I showed

Kurt where I would be sitting. I informed Kurt of some questions they would ask him and pretended I was the state attorney asking the questions.

Me: Kurt, your name is Kurt, right?

Kurt: Yes

Me: And how old are you, Kurt?

Kurt: Five

Me: Do you know why we are here today?

Kurt: Yes

Me: Can you tell me why you think we are here?

Kurt: Because Daddy hurt me

Me: That's right. And do you see Daddy here today?

All at once, Kurt stopped and looked me straight in the eyes. I could see the terrified look in them when he suddenly asked, "Will Jim be there?"

My response was an honest "yes" to my visibly shaken son.

"Well, I don't want to see him," he replied.

Kurt and I talked about it for a while, and throughout he was adamant he did not want to see or be in the same room with Jim. Well, that was all I had to hear. I called the SAO the next day.

"Hi, how are you and Kurt doing?" the assistant state attorney asked.

"We are fine, but I'm afraid I have some bad news for you. Kurt will not testify at Jim's trial. Last night I performed a mock trial to show him what would happen in the courtroom. He asked me if Jim would be there, and I told him he would. Kurt then told me he didn't want to see Jim and would not do it."

"Was Kurt that shaken up?"

"Yes, he was." And I continued on my son's defense, "So, after Kurt went through all that violence, I will not, under any circumstances, force Kurt to see that monster again!"

"I understand. However, if Kurt does not testify, then the best we can try to get will be a plea agreement. Are you okay with that?" he asked.

"I guess it is going to have to suffice because I will not make Kurt see Jim again. I can't believe our system can let criminals like Jim get away with this! I'm sorry, I'm just upset. I'm not angry with you. Tell me, what do we do next?" I asked.

He responded, "First thing is, keep this between you and me. Do not, under any circumstances, tell anyone that Kurt will not testify. If you do and it gets back to Jim's attorney, there won't even be a plea deal. Understand?"

"Yes, of course."

"I will proceed as if the trial is going to take place. I will offer them a plea deal and appeal to them not to force Kurt to testify. If they accept, then that will be it."

"What if they don't agree?"

"That depends. They might not agree but counter with their own version of a plea deal. This is a negotiation, we offer something, and they accept or counter our offer. Then it continues until we either have an agreement or one of us pulls out of the negotiations. I don't want you to worry. We'll make this plea deal happen, okay?"

"Okay, thanks," I answered, feeling broken.

About a month later, late August 1991, the assistant state attorney called me again.

"Hello?"

"Hello, Diann. How are you and Kurt doing?"

"We are doing okay, a little better each day, although it's going to be a long haul. Have you got something for me?"

"Yes, I have some information for you. We have reached a tentative plea agreement if you approve. This plea agreement is the best we could do given the circumstances. As part of the plea agreement, he will receive probation, have counseling, no alcohol consumption, and must pay for counseling for you and Kurt, all for a one-year period."

"It really sucks that Jim is basically getting away with this. He goes and almost kills my son, and because of a judge's ruling, he goes scot-free. This is such a screwed-up system! I understand and just want him to stay far away from us and never contact us again. Hopefully, he doesn't end up killing a child down the road."

"I understand your frustration, but it's the best we can do. There is one more thing. I would like you to write a letter to the judge, a victim impact statement. If you could write that and get to me as soon as possible, we still have a trial date of September thirtieth."

"I'll start on that letter tonight and get it to you as soon as possible. So then, on September thirtieth, this nightmare with him will finally end? Except, of course, all the psychological repercussions Kurt and I are dealing with."

"Yes, Diann, this part of the nightmare will finally be over. Take care, and I'll be looking for that letter."

With that, our conversation was over, but I was livid at the thought Jim was getting away with what he did to Kurt.

There sure would have been a different outcome had Kurt been able to stand trial. But there was NO way I was going to make my baby stand trial and be in the same room as that demon. We took what we got and held our heads high.

Jim was convicted by Plea, two counts of Child Abuse with adjudication withheld. At least with his record, if he did abuse another child, the record was there. Now, we were finally free to continue our lives without this black cloud over our heads. Life could now go on.

***

Kurt and I started counseling immediately. I called several counseling offices until I found one that specialized in child abuse cases. The counselor we picked was a middle-aged female that both Kurt and I were comfortable with. At each session, she always greeted us with a warm smile and a calm, soothing demeanor. During our first visit, she said, "I understand the two of you went through quite a traumatic event in Florida. Would you care to share? Mom…Kurt?"

Kurt spoke right up. He told her everything that happened with Jim. He even went into detail about Jim following us and how he scared Mommy. Kurt didn't hesitate one bit. He sat there and said it all. He sure made me proud. It was as if he knew how important it was to speak about these events and how it would help him in the long run. How did a five-year-old comprehend this?

"Mom, you must be very proud of your son. I'd like to also have a private session with you next week if that can be arranged."

I know she wanted to discuss these incidents in more detail and to know how I was doing. I'm sure she didn't want to ask about certain details in front of Kurt. With my permission, she also scheduled private sessions with Kurt.

My private sessions came as a relief. Although I grew up here in Maine, I had no proper support system. Sure, I had a few girlfriends that would listen, but they didn't understand the grief I was going through. Unfortunately, or fortunately, they didn't understand what I needed. Unless someone has been abused, they truly do not understand.

"How can I help you, Diann?" the counselor asked in my next session, alone.

"I still fear Jim is going to come and find us, even though we live so far away. He had a habit of finding Kurt and me, even after we moved into another place, and it was very scary knowing he could do that. The fear is so real. I relive those days every day, even now, sixteen hundred miles away from him. I'm constantly looking over my shoulder in fear he may be near us again. I am so sick and tired of feeling this way. I'm having panic attacks. When will it ever stop?"

The counselor had such an outstanding bedside manner. She assured me the more we talked about Jim and all that had happened, the more comfortable I would feel. She told me it would take quite some time to feel at ease with all that had happened to us, especially since it was still so fresh. The counselor said the best thing to do was to keep up with my counseling sessions and suggested I keep a diary of my feelings, so I could purge daily. I was diagnosed with PTSD. I didn't feel comfortable being "labeled," but at least it made sense to me.

"I feel so guilty for what happened to Kurt. I can't get it out of my mind. If I just stayed home that night, he wouldn't have gone through any of that. If I'd never gone back to live with Jim every time he abused me," I told the counselor in another session.

"I understand your guilt, Diann. However, it

wasn't your fault. It was Jim's fault. It wasn't you who abused Kurt. He was the one who abused your son. You have caregiver's guilt. I understand as mothers we always feel responsible for our children."

"I honestly never felt Jim would have hurt Kurt. He always played well with him and never raised his voice with him, never had he scolded him. He left the scolding up to me. He never gave me any indication he would abuse him in any way. Ever. The night I was with my father, the night Kurt was abused, I left him alone with Jim and his daughter. Never in my wildest imagination would I have thought this would have happened. I'm not sure I will ever be free of this guilt."

"I'm sorry you are feeling this way. Let's work on these feelings for the next few sessions."

She always had a way to soothe me. At this point in my life, she sure was my saving grace. Thank God I was going to counseling. I had so many mixed emotions daily that many times alone at night, I felt like such a failure. But thanks to counseling, and my particular counselor, I could see there would be light at the end of the tunnel.

Kurt and I went to our sessions every week. I could see Kurt coming alive once again. It only took him a few months before I saw a complete change in my bright young boy. He was acting like a happy five-year-old. Knowing he felt better reassured me he was breaking free. I was trying to learn to deal with the guilt.

Kurt was becoming more and more relaxed in our new life. He was doing extremely well in school, made friends easily, and loved to ride his bike and play video games. He was interested in Cub Scouts, so he joined and started earning his badges right away.

Teachers enjoyed Kurt as he was a quick learner and usually was at the top of his class. His teachers told me, "Kurt doesn't have any problem with his schoolwork. He typically will receive one hundred percent on most assignments. The only downfall, if you will, Kurt quickly gets bored in class, and we can't keep him challenged. He races to the finish line with his schoolwork."

Kurt typically wanted to be number one with anything he was involved in, so sometimes, it created problems with his friends. Yet another thing to work on in counseling.

When I started feeling a little braver, I sat at my computer and purged my feelings and wrote a letter. Not just any letter; this was *the letter*. A letter to my family about the rape that I had suffered at the hands of my uncle. I think it started more as a journal, but then it occurred to me, why not send this out to the entire family and let in on the family secret my parents and I had been keeping.

I wrote what Uncle Sal had done to me, how it's made me feel, and how I felt the day I was writing the letter. Unfortunately, in all the moves I've made through the years, the letter was lost. I sent the letter to everyone in the family whose address I had. I mailed them out the next day.

I had put the word out. It felt exhilarating. I was anxious to know what they were going to say to me. I was frightened, not knowing what Uncle Sal might do. But, best of all, I felt good I used my voice.

No one responded to me. Not one person of all the people I sent the letter to. Not one word. So, basically, I wasn't acknowledged. Yet again. However, twenty years later, my grandmother (my mom's stepmom) wrote me a sweet note acknowledging that "back in those years," people didn't know how to respond or what to do. They didn't "talk" about those types of things, but that she believed me and she loved me. When I opened the card and read her words, tears flowed from my eyes. Finally, an acknowledgment.

***

Kurt and I were living basically a harmonious life. I worked at a management consulting firm as an office manager doing well for myself, and had a loving home with everything either of us wanted, although from time to time, we had our downtimes with our memories of Jim.

I became involved with Kurt's sports of baseball, basketball, and soccer. I became the secretary of the PTA and was a volunteer at United Way, which made it possible for me to meet many friends, which also helped me to keep my anxious feelings at bay about being stalked.

PART THREE

BETTER DAYS AHEAD

CHAPTER 10

Finding Happiness

IN 1992, I DIALED Joe's beeper and tapped in my phone number. It couldn't have been twenty minutes before I received a phone call.

"Hi, there! About time you sent me your phone number!" I could sense the smile on Joe's face.

"Yeah, sorry it's been so long, but I've been going through a lot getting settled in, counseling, and my new job. But it's great to hear your voice." I felt bad it was about a year since I had spoken with Joe, but I honestly needed some time before getting in touch with him.

"So, what's up?" Joe asked me right away.

I told him all about my job. "I really like it there. There are only three people who work at this office, and it feels like family. How about you?"

"Well, it's still the same 'ole thing working at the station. I've been keeping myself busy working overtime and as many details as I can. I really miss you. How is Kurt doing?" he asked.

"He's doing well. He seems to have bounced back to a carefree kid and doing fantastic in school. He has been taking part in sports. You'd be proud of him. And I miss you too." My heart ached. It was amazing how even six years later, my love for him hadn't diminished one bit.

***

The following year, Kurt and I were planning a trip to Florida to visit my mother. I sent an e-mail to Joe about my plans, and he immediately responded we had to see one another while I was there.

After we arrived in Fort Lauderdale, Joe and I met for lunch. I was excited to see him once again. I dressed in my favorite yellow flowered dress with white-and-gold sandals. Kurt stayed with my mother for the day, swimming in the pool her apartment sported.

"Hi!" I was practically screaming at Joe as I got out of my car. He was parked one row from me.

"It's really you. I can't believe it!" Joe replied.

We immediately embraced. An embrace that seemed to have lasted forever. I didn't want to let go. "We better get inside before we get kicked out of this parking lot for too much public display of affection," Joe said jokingly.

We entered Denny's hand in hand. I was on cloud nine. As we walked to our table, it felt as if others were watching us walk in. Was it the smiles on our faces and the electricity between the two of us folks were noticing? Or did I imagine it?

We talked candidly. "Diann, I wanted you to know I still care very much. I don't want you to forget that." He reached for my hand, and yet I pulled back a bit. "I know you live far away, and right now, we can't do anything about it. I just wanted to let you know." With those words, my eyes filled with tears.

"Joe, you will never know just how much I love you. It really hurts we live so far away from one another, but I know you understand why. I miss you so much." Joe started crying. He and I were now an emotional mess inside the restaurant.

The server came by at that moment and asked, "Would you like to order now?"

By the look on her face, I could see she knew she interrupted something. We placed our order and held hands across the table. Lunch was wonderful, but my stomach was so tight I could hardly eat. Joe chowed down, but it was more like eating for survival than enjoying his food.

The server came with the check, and Joe paid the bill. We had to part once again. Kurt and I would only stay in the area for a few more days, and Joe had to work, so there wouldn't be another opportunity to see one another again. As Joe and I embraced in the parking lot, we did not want to let go. He gave me a long kiss, one he knew would have to last until we saw each other again. I felt safe in that kiss and in his embrace.

The agony. The pain. *Why do we keep doing this to one another?*

Kurt and I returned to Maine, and our lives would return to their normal cadence. I would go to work each day while Kurt went to school. Kurt had his sports, and I would always be in attendance to watch his games. I had my PTA meetings, and we would have our events. I would go out on weekend nights while a friend of mine babysat. Week after week, this was our lives.

Joe and I continued our e-mails and phone calls to one another for a few years. Then in 1996, Joe and I were talking on the phone when suddenly I heard the words I yearned for since the day we met.

"I want to live the rest of my life with you," he told me over the phone that evening. It stunned me. Did I hear him correctly? Was I dreaming?

We talked about various possibilities how we were going to make this happen. He spoke of the possibility that after he retired from the police department in another five years, we could then get married. *Ugh...I don't want to wait that long!* Here we go again.

In July 1997, I planned another trip to Florida to spend time with Joe. We filled it with breathtaking moments. I was fortunate enough to spend more time with him than on the last visit. Joe and I took a drive to the beach and stayed for the day, enjoying the sun and sand between our toes. One day we took a drive to his mom's house. It had been quite a while since I had seen her. It was long overdue that I visited. Another day we went shopping. I wanted to purchase some souvenirs from the local shops. Seemed funny, as I used to live there, but I wanted to pick up a few things for my friends in Maine.

On the last day of our time together, we took a drive to Naples. When we arrived, we had lunch and did a little shopping. Later driving, Joe and I began discussing our future again. *Yes! This is what I want to talk about!*

"Diann, I love you so much. I think we need to revisit our plans. I don't want to wait until I retire to marry you." My heart was skipping beats when I heard those words again.

As we drove, he found a lovely park and parked the car under a beautiful palm tree. Joe took hold of my hands and looked straight into my eyes.

"How can we make this work? I know you moved back to Maine because you needed to get away from Jim, somewhere you and Kurt would be safe." Joe took a deep breath. "It's been six years now. Do you think you would be comfortable moving back?" Those words made me gasp, like sour grapes stinging my throat. I never had thought of that before.

"Joe, what about the possibility of you moving to Maine?"

"I'd move up there in a heartbeat. You know I love the cold and the snow, but I'm so close to retirement, I just can't do it right now. So, if I move to Maine, it wouldn't be until I retired."

I sat quietly for a few moments, thinking of how this transition would affect Kurt and me if we moved to Florida. "I need to talk to Kurt about this and get his feelings on it."

"I can completely understand that," Joe replied without hesitation.

"I know you do, Joe. It would be great for me to move back here, but I have to consider how Kurt would feel. If I moved back to Florida, what are you thinking the timeframe of this move would be?" I was itching to know his thinking.

"Well, whenever you wanted to would be fine with me. We would plan on a day, I'd fly up, rent a truck, and move you guys down. I would drive the truck, and you could follow me in the car." I was getting excited to hear this idea.

I spoke to Kurt and my mother that evening about what Joe and I discussed. I could sense that Kurt didn't have any qualms about the idea. He told me he liked Joe and would like it if we all lived together. Knowing that, I was delirious.

Starting in August, Joe flew up to Maine from Florida about every other weekend. It was wonderful. We took drives to the mountains, went to Acadia National Park, and visited lighthouses. We tried to spend as much quality time together as we could. Joe also spent some time getting to know Kurt one-on-one. They played catch football, went to the park, played basketball, and there were also Kurt's video games. At night, Joe and I would go to the Holiday Inn, dance, and talk with my friends. I introduced Joe to several of them, and they all became like family.

On October 11, 1997, Joe reserved a hotel room for the weekend. He thought some alone time was due for the two of us. Joe proposed to me in room 228 at the Holiday Inn. He took both my hands, looked me in my eyes, and asked me, "Diann, you make me the happiest man on earth. I have loved no one as much as I love you. We have gone through so much together, and I don't want to waste any more time. Will you marry me and make me the happiest man on earth?"

With tears streaming down my eyes, I was speechless. All I could do was nod.

Joe then slipped the beautiful marquise diamond ring on my left finger. I couldn't believe it. After eleven long years, we finally came to the point in our lives to decide to get married. We were elated.

Joe continued to visit every other weekend from Florida, and we started planning for Kurt and my move back to Florida, the first weekend in January 1998. God had finally smiled on us.

***

Joe and I had plans to be married on August 16, 1998.

The anniversary of the day we met twelve years prior.

Kurt and I had been living with Joe for three months, and Kurt was enjoying his sports. He enjoyed ice-skating at the local inside rink. He decided he wanted to play ice hockey, so we would take him to the rink and drop him off. He had a terrible fall, and we had to take him to the ER. Kurt and I didn't have health insurance. I wasn't working, and since Joe and I weren't married yet, we were not on his insurance policy. Joe and I had another decision to make. Should we get married earlier to have insurance? Just in case?

We discussed it and decided we could not take a chance on either Kurt or I ending up in the hospital and not being able to afford the cost. We decided on April 23, we would get married. A minister at Joe's mom's house performed the ceremony. We were outside by the lovely, fresh-smelling white gardenias. Kurt was by my side.

After the "I do's" were said, I was gleaming. I was extremely happy. Finally, the day had come when I was Joe's wife. It almost didn't seem real, as I had been waiting for so long. It had been almost twelve years since we had met. True love sure does wait.

Our marriage had its strains. Being married to law enforcement wasn't always easy. The stress of police work takes its toll on family life and can certainly disrupt the normal flow of any marriage. A police officer's marriage, like any other marriage, needs a strong foundation, trust, commitment, honesty, and a lot of patience for the spouse. A typical marriage takes work to keep strong and healthy. Add in strange hours, working on holidays and birthdays, court time, and being called in at all hours, which increases the stress level exponentially. The spouse needs to understand they will work with prostitutes, drug addicts, murderers, etc., and don't forget the possibility of those drive-by shootings. Oh yes, and of course, domestic disputes are well-known to be the most dangerous calls for police to respond to. If you feel you can handle this and much more and be the supportive spouse, you have a chance at having a healthy marriage with law enforcement. This wasn't always the case in our marriage.

Moving back to Florida had its pros and cons. I couldn't have been happier to live with Joe and be with him the rest of my life, don't get me wrong. However, it didn't take me long to feel triggered by memories of Jim stalking me once I arrived in the sunny state. I had learned that Jim was now living in a town close to where we were living.

My PTSD was coming back and getting worse. There would be times when I was home alone, I thought I saw Jim watching me through the windows or driving up the street back and forth. Just as I had lived through once before. I knew it all too well. It was etched deep into my memory. *He was never there.* PTSD at its finest. This went on for months and put a big strain on my day-to-day life. I needed counseling again, but I didn't reach out. Not for a while. Not soon enough.

When Joe had some rare days off we would go to the tennis court, and the three of us would play for a couple of hours. We'd have a great time not playing by the rules, of course! Just hitting the ball back and forth the best we could. Chasing the ball, more like it! Kurt would get a kick out of it and make fun of us for "being too old" to play and to keep up with him. We would go to the basketball court, and Joe and Kurt would play hoops for an afternoon. We might end the day at Dairy Queen and get ice cream and enjoy it on the bench in the warm Florida afternoon. On Friday nights, Joe and I would get Chinese food, and Kurt would get pizza. The three of us would rent a movie, and that would be our ritual each and every week. Nice family time.

But then would come those nights that Joe and I would have our conversations alone. And my insecurities would peak. My thoughts about Dick and Jim would rise. My memory of how they treated me and how they perceived me to be acting made me feel as though Joe would feel the same way. I worried that when Joe was at work, he would be with other women. My problem always was my insecurities from my past relationships. They led to arguments. Not always would Joe be able to keep me calm, to say the least. There were times when Joe would have to hold me or even shake me to make me realize what I was saying. Never during my marriage did I not feel safe with Joe. I never felt he would hurt me, and he never has, nor will he. Because I felt safe, I always felt comfortable in how I was arguing with him. My memories brought out the worst in me. Sometimes these arguments were ugly. Just nasty. And they all stemmed from my unresolved issues.

There was one night the argument got so bad that he left me and went to his mother's house. He came back a few days later. It was at that time he said we had to go to counseling. During the first session, he was upset and informed me that if we ever fought as badly as we did that night, the marriage would be over. Our arguments were never as bad again.

Thankfully, the love Joe had for me kept our marriage together. He had the understanding that what I was saying to him was due to my past, that it was not directed at him. I'm not saying there weren't those arguments that weren't hard for him because there were. But because of his love, he never gave up on me.

I was also cleaning the house like crazy, feeling as though Joe would criticize me for it not being perfect like Dick did. This was ridiculous for me to feel this way. Never did Joe mention to me anything about my cleaning, but because Dick had instilled that into me for so long, it carried with me. Joe did mention to me why I was cleaning so much, and I eventually told him. He then told me to not worry about cleaning the house as I was; however, it took me a long time to not feel that way. You can't stop those feelings overnight.

My PTSD and anxiety were all playing a role in my day-to-day living.

We continued our counseling. We didn't feel the counselor we had was the best fit. He was young, and we didn't feel he had the experience necessary for the problems Joe and I were having. We should have changed to a different counselor, but this was the counselor that Kurt had been seeing, and Kurt felt comfortable with him. We felt the counselor would benefit from the information he received from the three of us.

Joe and I seemed to have worked through some issues after a few months, so we discontinued our sessions. I still needed counseling for my PTSD, but I didn't realize it at the time. I wasn't verbalizing my fears with Joe. When I was alone in the house, my panic attacks would continue, and my memories of Jim would still be there.

I was an instructional designer working for American Express. I was working from home, writing procedures, and could set my own hours. Mostly, I worked from eight to six, but there were many times I'd work late into the night. When Joe would be working long shifts, this gave me a chance to keep busy. Working at home made it possible to be available to Kurt if he ever needed me, which had its advantages. Whenever I needed to take Kurt to the doctor or dentist, I didn't need to take personal time off from work to do so. I just worked longer hours at home or on the weekend.

CHAPTER 11

Public Speaking

DURING KURT'S JUNIOR YEAR in high school, 2002, he was enrolled in a program that allowed him to go to college and graduate high school, simultaneously receiving his associate's degree, similar to the program I had gone through. However, Kurt would start the program in his junior year in high school instead of his senior year, as I did. He would live at home throughout the program. He would attend the local community college for his last two years of high school. With this program, tuition was paid free and clear, as well as books.

In 2003, during Kurt's senior year in high school in correlation with his second year of college, the State of Florida required students applying for state-sponsored scholarships to perform a specific number of hours volunteering in the community to qualify. He wanted to go on to college to earn his bachelor's degree but didn't want to have an enormous debt once he graduated. He could accomplish that. He just needed to keep his grades up. No problem there, as he always had all A's in his classes. We discussed various options for volunteering but couldn't quite decide.

We were both home one afternoon. Kurt and I were in the kitchen having a late lunch. I poured a cup of coffee and asked him, "Kurt, what do you think about volunteering at a domestic violence shelter? You have an up-close and personal knowledge of what domestic violence is, and I think that you can help many people. Would this be something you'd be interested in?" I could see that he was thinking about doing this.

"You know, Mom, I think I am going to call that organization Women in Distress of Broward County."

After calling the shelter and making an appointment to meet with an advocate, the two of us traveled a half hour to Ft. Lauderdale for the meeting. There was a lengthy discussion of the various volunteer options that were available to Kurt. There were many areas in which to volunteer, one of them being a speaker, speaking to high school students. Since Kurt had been abused, he could use his story to help assure other students who had been or were in similar situations that they are not alone and to show them there is a way out and to receive help when they need it.

Curious about this volunteering opportunity, I

wanted to become involved. I asked about volunteering also, and at the end of our meeting, we both signed up. So, mother and son became volunteers, working for the first time together! I spoke at churches, community events, and civic organizations, while Kurt spoke at high schools and churches.

At one of Kurt's speaking engagements, I stood behind the stage and listened to my baby. I was in tears throughout. I was proud to listen to this young man tell his story of abuse. He went on in detail about what Jim had done to him. He spoke profoundly to his young crowd, a crowd of his peers. I would peek out and see teens mesmerized, listening to him tell his story.

Yes, Kurt did a fine job. There was a part of me that was proud of him, yet another part of me wished there had never been a need for him to be there at all. I was still having a hard time getting rid of my guilt. This would be the only speaking engagement of his I could attend since he was speaking mostly during the day while I was working.

Kurt continued the speaking engagements for the specific number of hours he needed to complete the qualification for the college scholarships while I continued going forward. I thoroughly enjoyed this opportunity to tell others of my past domestic violence and informing them there was help available in their community. Education is key, and being a tool was useful for my therapy.

One of my first of many speaking engagements was at a mall in Pembroke Pines, Florida. I was nervous because I feared Jim could possibly be there, or even Rachel. However, I felt compelled to tell my story.

This speaking engagement was for the Clothesline Project. This project addresses violence against women by providing a vehicle for women to express their emotions by decorating a t-shirt.

When I arrived at the mall, there were over fifty decorated shirts. Each of the t-shirts was decorated by domestic violence victims or family/friends of those victims. The sight made me gasp. I was already feeling anxious because I was about to speak, but the reality sank in when I saw the shirts. I walked around, reading each shirt while waiting to speak. The leader of the project walked up to me and asked if I was the speaker for the day.

"Yes, I am Diann from Women in Distress. I'm looking forward to speaking here today."

"Well, we are very glad you could make it. As you know, it is very important to get the word out to the public regarding domestic violence. Are you going to tell your personal story of domestic violence, Diann?"

"Yes, and provide resources in Broward County."

"Perfect. Let me show you where you'll be speaking and get you acclimated. You have about five minutes. You may want to get up there and start preparing."

I was excited. "Let's go!" I said to her.

As I stepped up to the podium, my body was shaking. I needed to calm myself down. *Why are you shaking? You can do this. You've handled the worst already. You can share your story and help others. Get a grip.*

"Ladies and gentlemen, I'd like to introduce to you Diann Diaz. She is with Women in Distress and is here to speak to you about her personal domestic violence situation. Please join me with a warm welcome."

People in the crowd turned their attention in my direction.

"Thank you for inviting me here to speak today." I looked at the audience, and my stomach tightened. I grabbed onto the podium and began to speak. "Domestic violence is a horrible human atrocity."

The audience was looking at me with such intensity.

I told my story of being abused and of the struggle to break free and survive. I started with my ex-husband Dick and how he had abused and controlled me throughout our brief marriage. How it was hard to leave him and what I thought was love wasn't. How an alcoholic will drink and continue to drink, no matter how much they love someone. If they are violent with you, more often than not, they will not change. The black-and-blues not only affect you but also your family and friends who will worry and don't want to see you in such a horrific, detrimental relationship.

I shifted gears and spoke to them about Jim's abuse, to me and to Kurt. It was during this time I watched the crowd intently and saw people in the crowd crying.

As I completed my presentation, I wanted to leave them with information that could help them or someone they knew and loved.

I told the crowd, "If you or anyone you know is going through a domestic violence situation, sexual assault or child abuse, I want you to know there is help for you. Call Women in Distress or your local women's center. They can help lead you in the right direction. I know how scary it is for you. I was there once."

"Also, counseling is extremely important. Brushing it aside is not good and could have devastating consequences for you. Keeping it all bottled up, believe me, one day, it will harm other relationships you are in or even destroy them. It can even cause problems with your coworkers or boss, could lead to being disciplined or even fired. You may not realize it, but those feelings you are hiding affect everything you do."

"If you know of someone in an abusive relationship, talk to them. Ask them if they are ready to accept help. Just let them know you are always there for them when they are ready. Don't push them, as they may not come to you in the future. When the time comes, they will know you are there for them."

"Never say to a victim it's their fault or question them why they don't leave their partner. Questions like that can revictimize them and will be counterproductive, setting them back. They may not even know why they stay. Abusers are so controlling. Victims may be restricted to the home or not allowed to speak to their family or friends because abusers may feel the victim will tell someone about the abuse that is occurring."

The audience was staring.

"Often victims are afraid because they feel they have no place to go, their abuser may be the sole breadwinner in the family. They may fear not being able to survive if they can leave the abuser or have them arrested. All these concerns can be addressed by calling Women in Distress of Broward County. Let them help you."

I continued speaking at various localities with my personal story. It was soothing to know that if I helped just one person, then I had achieved something worthwhile.

A year later, Kurt and I were invited to the Speaker of the Year event. That year, Kurt and I both received the Speaker of the Year award from Women in Distress of Broward County, Florida, Speakers Bureau (2003-2004). We received framed certificates, and it was such an honor. But receiving this with Kurt was the ultimate honor. It was a proud moment and a vindication of all we had been through.

This was just the beginning of my volunteer work for domestic violence victims.

We transformed something so tragic in our own lives and have helped pave the way for others to find their voice.

CHAPTER 12

Changes & Losing Mom

IN 2004, KURT WAS accepted to the University of North Florida in Jacksonville, and he continued his studies in business to receive his bachelor's degree. When the day came to bring him to campus, my heart was breaking. My baby wouldn't be living with me anymore! Was I ready for this? Was he? Of course, he was, and I trusted him with my whole heart. It was me having a hard time letting my baby go. He was about to embark on a whole new life.

Joe and I traveled the four-hour drive with Kurt to the college campus and spoke about his upcoming opportunities. When we arrived, I felt I would break down and cry, but I held it together. We found his dorm and went inside to search for his room.

"It's a good size. Want me to make your bed?" I asked, barely keeping tears at bay.

"Sure, Mom. Go ahead," Kurt said with a grin.

Diann Diaz

He knew I was having a hard time with this transition, and I think he was just going along with my staggering words.

"Want me to put away your clothes?" I asked. This time he put his foot down.

"Mom, it's okay. I got this." I think he was ready for his mother to leave and start enjoying his freedom.

After talking for thirty minutes, I got the "look" from him and realized it was time. Joe looked at me, so I got the message. "Okay, guys, I get it. Let's go. Kurt, come outside with us to say goodbye?"

The three of us went outside to the back of his dorm, where we had parked our black Ford F-150, now empty of Kurt's belongings. My heart ached.

"Please call me once in a while and let me know how you are doing? I want to know what you are up to, how your classes are, and what you are doing for fun. Can you do that for me, hon?"

"Yes, Mom. I will keep in touch. I promise." I could see his eyes rolling toward Joe, and Joe laughed. *I don't see the humor.* As we left campus for the drive back home, the tears started flowing down my cheek. This was going to be a long drive.

As for Joe and me, we had big plans and changes of our own coming.

The prior summer, Joe started thinking about retiring. After many hours of discussion, we decided on Virginia as a place to call home. We had traveled there years earlier and found we loved it. So, we took a three-week vacation to Virginia to get an idea of where we would like to live.

By April 2004, Joe made the decision to retire from the police department. I can't say that it was unexpected when he brought it up. He had worked as an officer for almost twenty-five years. It was time. Joe still wanted to work, just not in South Florida. In May 2004, he put his resume on an internet website, looking for consultant work in Virginia.

We wanted to move, to get out of the hectic rat race that South Florida possessed. Within two weeks of Joe posting his resume, a police department in Virginia contacted him and was interested in hiring him.

This started us out driving to Southwest Virginia about every two weeks for the next three months. These trips were exhausting, a twelve-hour drive one way, and we had to make the trip in the three days Joe was off from work. Joe would have interviews and testing, then we would look for a new home.

Joe was told he was hired in July and was given a tentative start date from the end of September to the beginning of October. We put our home up for sale and continued traveling the long twelve hours to Virginia.

We finally found our home; however, it wasn't until after our umpteenth millionth trip to Virginia. We had returned home from a trip to Virginia when our realtor called us and stated she had found a 3600 sq. foot farmhouse that stood on twenty acres of land if we were interested. The following weekend we, once again, we were on the road to see the house. The center of the house, which was the original portion, was a wormy chestnut, two-story cabin that dated from the mid-1800s. The rest of the house was built around this portion of the home years later.

We were interested, put a bid on the home, and the next thing we knew, we were now owners of two homes. We still hadn't sold our home in Florida.

Of course, I wanted to share the twenty acres of land with horses, one feature we loved so much about our new home. I could have horses once again. Ever since being a young child, horses were important to me, as they provided such comfort. I never wanted to give that up, and now that I had the opportunity again, I was enthusiastic about starting once more.

The following summer, we drove four hours to an animal rescue shelter in Tennessee. Then we saw them. Diamond and Koko. Diamond was a dark chestnut, half Appaloosa and half-quarter horse gelding. He looked similar to the horse Mama I had when I was young. Koko was a white and gray half Appaloosa, half-quarter horse mare, with a short black mane. She was simply gorgeous, with a timid personality. Joe and I took them for a "test run," and after riding both of them, I knew I wanted them at home with me. Their gaits were perfect. I was in love.

We purchased both of them, and they were

delivered to us two weeks later. As the trailer was driving up our driveway, I was giggling like a child. I was excited! The driver stopped at the causeway entry of what is now to us our horse pathway. He opened the back of the trailer. First, Diamond made his presence known as he whinnied his discourse for being locked in the truck for so long. Then came Koko. She stomped her front hoof on the grassy knoll of the path and looked right at Diamond. Her expression was priceless. It was as though she asked him with her eyes, "where the hell are we?" then looked at the landmass around her and let out a long, hard "nay!" Diamond followed her lead, and in my heart of hearts, I knew they were home.

I was in heaven—finally. I had horses in my life once again. I had the time and the opportunity to dedicate most of my days to riding. My anxiety and PTSD were at bay, and I was happy again.

***

At the end of August in 2005, I received a phone call from my mother stating she hadn't been feeling well. She was complaining of major back pain and said she wasn't able to perform her job as a cashier well. Her boss was allowing her to use a bar stool to complete her work at the Publix shopping center in Davie, Florida.

"Mom, if it's that bad, go to the doctor and get it checked out."

"I know. I was just hoping it would go away." She never liked going to the doctor, but this time I could hear in her voice it scared her.

"Mom, please set up an appointment as soon as you can and let me know how it goes."

A week later, she called me to inform me she had an MRI on her back. The results came back stating she had a large mass on her uterus, and she needed to make an appointment with an oncologist.

A few days later, Mom was feeling worse and went to the ER. A few hours later, the hospital called me. They informed me she was in kidney failure, and they would like to operate but needed my permission. I agreed to the surgery. I immediately packed a bag and drove from Virginia to Florida. Joe had to stay and work but informed me he would drive to Florida if need be.

I arrived at my mother's small apartment at three o'clock in the morning. Five hours later, I rushed to the hospital. Her doctor was just making the rounds.

"Hi, Doc. I'm Catherine's daughter, Diann. Can you inform me of her status? What's going on?"

"Well, we had to remove one of her kidneys, and she seems to be recovering well."

"What about the mass she has in her uterus? What are you going to do about that?"

"Her body won't be able to tolerate another surgery." Shortly afterward, the doctor left the room.

With that information, my heart dropped. The

doctor informed me the size of her mass was the size of a football.

Her hospital stay consisted of a week. I was at the hospital all day and would not leave until ten o'clock at night to be with her as long as I could. I would sit in the room with her for hours, then take a break occasionally and sit in the family room down the hall. In the meantime, she received a few visitors from work. There were three phone calls from family.

A week later, she was strong enough to be transported to rehab. As she was getting comfortable in her new "suite," I was glancing at the new set of nurses who were going to be taking care of her. We were just waiting to see what was going to happen to her at this point. Waiting to see how her only kidney held up. Would she be able to have her mass removed? The docs had already performed tests, and it was cancer. How much time did my mom have left on this earth? Could they help her? All these questions in my mind, but no one knew the answers. It was now all up to God.

She rested comfortably at the rehab for only a week when trouble again appeared. Her only kidney became infected, she was weak, and the meds she was being given did not help. The rehab rushed her back to the hospital.

"What's going on? What can be done, Doc?" I asked with fear in my voice.

"Diann, I'm sorry. There isn't anything we can

do. We will keep her comfortable for a few days and see if the infection clears up. She is weakening. We may need to transfer her to hospice. I want you prepared."

With that news, I felt gloom. My mother was going to die? What? So quickly? It was only a couple of weeks ago her back was hurting. How could this be? It was two days later when she was transferred to hospice. I rode with her in the bumpy ambulance to the hospice, which was only five miles away.

The next morning, I called my brother Stephen in Indiana and told him that Mom was in hospice and we needed to prepare for her death. I was going to be calling a funeral home and get the information for her to be cremated since this was Mom's wish.

In the meantime, Mom was in tremendous pain, that they had her on a lot of morphine she could barely talk. My days of speaking to Mom were over. I stayed the rest of the day. It was a quiet day. That evening at seven, I left to go to Mom's apartment. I sat on her bed and cried. I loved Mom. We had a rough go at it for years, but she was still my mother.

It was September 14 when I received the phone call at three thirty in the morning. It was the hospice nurse informing me my mother had passed away. I told them I would be right there. I dressed quickly, got in the truck, and rushed to my mother's side.

After going to the funeral home and making all the necessary arrangements, I felt I had nowhere to go and didn't want to go back to my mom's place any time soon. I drove up and down familiar A1A along the beach to clear my mind. It was soothing for me to breathe in the salt air. With the sun so warm and my windows rolled down, it was a welcome relief from the past three weeks. I was sad my mom had passed, but she was in such pain, it was best she passed. I didn't want her suffering anymore.

Two hours later, I drove back to my mother's apartment. As hard as it was, I cleaned out her things. I boxed up her clothing and donated them to Goodwill. Then it was time to box items I wanted to keep. As I perused through her drawers, I came upon a few items I remembered as a child, some photo albums and pictures my son had made her in years past. All went home with me.

The next day, I packed my truck with her belongings I kept and hit the road for the twelve-hour drive back home. The memories of my mother were thoughts of mine during my travel. All the years of drama. How I wished things could have been different while growing up. How I wished my mother would have been a happier person and could have known her daughter Cindi who she lost through the court system. I realized one thing. Mom was her own person. She kept to herself and lived her own life. That was her decision, and there wasn't anything I could have done to change that. I sure wish my mom had been a better communicator so I could have learned more about her before she died at seventy.

Once I was home a few days, I called my father to give him the news of Mom. He gave his sympathies and left it at that. No other discussions were had.

CHAPTER 13

Women's Resource Center

A YEAR AND A half after moving to Virginia, I became itchy to do something in the community. I had been cooped up in our home for much too long. Joe was a detective, working every day and getting called out numerous nights during the week, leaving me home alone. I decided to volunteer for domestic violence once again. I researched for a local women's shelter and found there was a Women's Resource Center only thirty minutes from our home and in the same town where Joe worked.

I called the women's center and made an appointment to visit the supervisor the following Wednesday and learned there were a few volunteer options I could choose from.

I went to the next volunteer training session, which was a few weeks later. My plan was to become a speaker with the volunteers, as a survivor offering my experiences to the attendees so they would be better equipped when being with victims, and become an emergency advocate, which is responding to victims of sexual assault or domestic violence 24/7 at the hospital or the police station.

I started my first speech with the following training session.

The conference room was set up with multiple long tables that easily accommodated the twenty-five people who were there, male and female. Most of these individuals were young college students. Some were older women wanting to help in the community.

My speeches often started with a photograph of Kurt at age four. I took the 8x10 photograph of Kurt out of my bag. It was a school picture of him when he was in a Montessori school. He had on a blue-and-white shirt with his arms crossed. He looked so cute with his blond hair and a small grin. As I placed it on the whiteboard, I could hear the students say, "aww."

I welcomed them to the training and introduced myself, telling them I was new to the area and I was a speaker in Florida. I explained to them how I broke the cycle of abuse with my child, at the hands of the man I loved. I would leave the photograph up throughout my presentation so they could view it while I discussed the history of events.

"I noticed you responded to this young boy. This is my son when he was four years old. I have a story to share with you." With that, I told them about my past and how I met Jim. It continued how Jim abused me and that ugly night when Jim abused Kurt.

Mesmerized trainees listened to me and began to tear up. I could see their eyes and mouths wide open. It was difficult for me to look at those so touched by my words, as it often brought me to tears. I had to stay strong, just as I did as a child. I was still beating myself up at times, as the guilt would still hit me from time to time, especially when I spoke about Kurt's abuse.

After the class was complete and before evaluations were turned in, a few of the trainees would have questions. "Why did you leave and then go back?" "How did you get through each abusive situation?"

"I didn't leave in the beginning because I felt as though Jim would change. After each time he'd hit me, he would be so kind to me and act as if he'd never do it again. I thought I loved him at the time and trusted him. Boy, was I wrong. But this is why I stayed. Obviously, I had no self-esteem and didn't like myself very much. I also believe that stems from not learning what a healthy relationship looked like when I was young. I never was taught that it isn't okay for someone to treat me in this manner. I was raised in a home where there was yelling and screaming all the time, and my father let my mother get away with it. My mother verbally abused us kids, and Dad did nothing about it. This is what I learned. I knew nothing else. As an adult, I thought this behavior was the norm. Until my son was abused. I would not stand for anyone hurting my child. That is when the cycle would end. That is when my assertiveness started. I also didn't know of any women shelters in the area. I didn't know there were places for me to seek help."

Everyone was listening intently.

"As far as how I got through each abusive situation and the black-and-blues, it was in my mind he loved me, and this would stop. There were a lot of tears along the way, and he had made many promises. There were many clouds in my life."

Most classes ended with trainees coming to me at the end of class, stating they were glad I finally left and appreciated my speaking at the training. With those words, it made it all worthwhile. If there was one person in that training that may be going through what I had gone through and listened to how I got out, it was all worth it. Also, these attendees would be helping those in the community, so listening to me would hopefully help those they would meet.

A few months followed, and the director of the women's center asked me to become a board member.

"What does this entail?"

"We have meetings once a month, and we'd like input from you regarding various issues at the center we discuss throughout the year," stated the director.

"Of course, I'd be honored!"

I was a board member for the following year, all the while I was volunteering until they asked me to become a staff member.

In the meantime, I embraced the training to become an emergency advocate. This volunteer work was intense. I'd be called out in all hours of the night. It was mostly to the hospitals for victims of sexual assault, and at times for domestic violence victims. I would be in the forensic room with them during their exams. This would consist of me sitting with the victim, holding their hand, comforting them during the forensic exam, explaining step-by-step the process of what would happen next. I would also be there to inform them of the local resources available.

At times, I would also be in the waiting room, informing families of the victim about local resources. Family members may never have known about sexual assault or domestic violence, may or may not know the right thing to say, as I experienced as a child and young adult.

I felt I was in an excellent position for this advocacy work because of my history of violence and having the ability to empathize with the victims and their families. The age ranges of victims I had been with were two to sixty years old. I can't imagine how many victims I accompanied. Well over 200.

I became a full-time staff member as the peaceline coordinator at the Women's Resource Center in January 2007. I thought this would help my depression and boost my self-esteem, as it gave me more responsibilities than just volunteering. My position handled the violence prevention education curriculum and presentations throughout the schools, sixth through tenth grades, on behalf of this domestic violence and sexual assault crisis center. I conducted approximately 500+ presentations to approximately 4000 students per school year, scheduling presentations in schools and the community, creating and updating educational violence prevention material. All while still being on call as an emergency advocate and conducting my personal speeches at training sessions.

I thoroughly enjoyed this job. The kids were fantastic. Sure, there were those children that didn't pay attention in class, their heads bowed to the desk, some eyes would roll when I spoke, but I chalked it up to the fact that they were still listening. And who knew? Maybe they were being abused at home, and this subject was difficult for them to hear. I let them off the hook.

Knowing I was making a difference in the lives of these children and educating them on violence prevention, which was never an opportunity in my day, was exhilarating.

But the job had its hard days, too. One tough piece was when after class, a child would walk up to me and inform me they had been sexually assaulted or abused at home in other ways, and they wanted help. Such sad situations. Such brave kids.

These children would inform me of what

happened to them at home by a trusted adult. They were abused by a neighbor, a minister, a family friend, or one of their parents.

One day, a young girl approached me. "Mrs. Diaz, can I speak to you?" the ten-year-old girl with dimples asked as she walked up to me after class.

"Of course you can. What can I do for you, Nora?"

"I was listening in class, and you said that if we needed help with something, we could talk to you. Right?"

"Of course you can. Do you need help?"

"I think so. This is hard for me to tell you," she said with her head low. I could tell she was scared. She shook. "My neighbor. Well, he. He's touching me in places he's not supposed to, and I'm too afraid to tell anyone about it. I think it's wrong because it doesn't make me feel good. I'm scared. What should I do?" My heart ached for this child.

"Well, first of all, I'm very proud of you for telling me this. I know it wasn't easy. And, it isn't your fault what is happening, do you understand?" A slight nod bounced from her head, with her eyes reaching my eyes. "Let's go to the guidance counselor and have a little chat. We will go from there. I will be with you, okay?"

"Okay. Am I in trouble?"

"Of course not! You did an amazing job by telling me! I'm proud of you!" We then walked to the guidance office and waited for the counselor to speak with us. It must have seemed like a lifetime for her, as it did for me. I was proud of this young lady.

"How can I help you?" the guidance counselor asked.

"Hi. I'm Diann Diaz and am the peaceline coordinator of the Women's Resource Center. I have Nora, and she told me something I feel she needs to tell you, as well." The guidance counselors were fully aware if I brought a child to them, it must mean they are being abused in some manner. She gave me a look of understanding, and we entered her office and sat down on her couch.

Nora told the guidance counselor exactly what she told me. She then went into more detail, saying that this neighbor was at her house often during the week, as he was a friend of her father's.

The counselor would then make a phone call to Child Protective Services and inform them of the situation. Depending on the severity of the case, the police may be called to come to the school to talk to the child. Those cases were rare, but if it was a parent abusing the child, that is when those situations generally arose.

My job was finished with the child at that point. The guidance counselor would take over and would follow up with the child, and CPS and/or the police would handle the case from there.

Nora wasn't the only child who came to me after

class. She was one of many. I gave these children so much credit for the bravery they exhibited to seek an adult for help. To trust anyone with that information is hard for an adult, let alone a child. My words helped them use their voice? *Wow!*

After about a year and a half, an opportunity to become the Sexual Assault Coordinator, and I applied for it and was granted the position.

I was responsible for the public education programs pertaining to sexual assault. I conducted 250+ presentations to approximately 2000 students/community members per year, recruited and trained the emergency advocate volunteers, coordinated scheduling of emergency advocates, supervised emergency advocates, provided effective sexual assault outreach programs in the community, provided in-service training for other allied professionals in the community, and maintained a working relationship with area hospitals, law enforcement agencies, universities and community colleges.

I continued to respond to requests for counseling to victims of sexual assault as needed and provided follow-up services with victims who were provided services by an emergency advocate. I was still on call a certain number of nights during the month for any sexual assaults or domestic violence cases; plus, if a volunteer called out sick or didn't respond, I was responsible to take the call.

As needed, I was also responding to the Children's Advocacy Center. A Children's Advocacy Center is a child-focused, facility-based program where representatives from many disciplines meet to discuss and make decisions about investigation, treatment, intervention, and prosecution of child abuse cases. They also work together to prevent further victimization of children.

The multidisciplinary team approach brings together under one umbrella all the professionals and agencies needed to offer comprehensive services: law enforcement, child protective services, prosecution, mental health, medical, and victim advocacy.

Here locally, when a case of child abuse was reported and law enforcement is involved, they are mandated to contact Child Protective Services. Then the investigation continues as a criminal investigation conducted by the police. The child welfare investigation will be conducted by CPS to assess the child's risk and/or need for removal from the home. As part of the criminal investigation, the police, in conjunction with CPS, would make arrangements with the CAC to interview the child.

Children would be sent to the Children's Advocacy Center to be interviewed about the abuse they endured. They were questioned by specially trained CPS, law enforcement, or child development personnel. While they were being interviewed, they were being videotaped for potential use during a court proceeding. There was a one-way mirror where a team member would watch and interject questions they might need answering. My job during this time was to be with the parent or family member that had brought them to the advocacy center. They would not be in the interview room with the child. I would provide comfort and information regarding resources in the community and help keep their mind off of where they actually were. It certainly wasn't easy for a parent to be in this building, knowing their child had been abused, and that child was a few feet away, being interviewed. I would let them talk to me about the abuse if they wanted.

Sometimes there were no family members with the child, so I would sit in the private, one-way mirrored room, watching and listening to the child being interviewed. That was my first mistake. Watching and listening to how that child had been abused. Watching through the one-way mirror, seeing a child in a colorful room, sitting in a blue chair, possibly displaying with a few dolls to explain their assault. That child's voice is one of the saddest, most depressing sounds anyone can listen to.

I overworked myself constantly, and the worst part of it was, that was the worst thing for me to do for myself and the victims. You need to take care of yourself first before taking care of others. My PTSD was spiking.

As time went on in this position, the negative

aspects wore on me. My depression worsened, I barely slept, and my relationships with others became challenging. I could feel myself being short with people at work, and my relationship with Joe was dwindling. We argued constantly. I was in pain and didn't realize it.

I had the opportunity in 2007 and 2008 to present at the Southwest Virginia Regional Conference on Domestic Violence in Abington and reached approximately 200 professionals in Virginia. I designed my own program, "Domestic Violence Victims—Why Do They Stay." This workshop gave an understanding, from the point of view of a survivor, of why many victims of domestic violence stay with their abusers. They learned techniques to help victims become survivors.

My personal story was requested many times from the local colleges and universities and other areas in the community. I enjoyed speaking at the colleges, as I was speaking to the younger adults and was hoping to grasp their attention before they entered serious relationships.

One presentation was in a remote area of Virginia, and I felt it was important for me to be there presenting, as there wasn't a lot of information about abuse in that community. This was on October 30, 2008, which I was the guest speaker at the Citizens Against Family Violence vigil. Here again, t-shirts with messages of support for violence victims hung about. There were only about thirty in attendance, but for this community, as small as it was, the turnout impressed me. All stood in the cold evening in warm coats and scarves, which told me they felt it was important to be there. I hoped my voice reached at least one person to help them receive the help they deserved.

CHAPTER 14

Emergency Advocacy

Sexual Assault

IT WAS THREE O'CLOCK on a Sunday morning, and my pager was vibrating on my nightstand. It was time to rise and shine and call the Crisis Hotline. Someone had been raped, or a domestic violence dispute had taken place in my local community. I was the emergency advocate on-call that week, so I had to accompany the victim to the hospital or the police station. Emergency advocates are trained volunteers who are on-call around the clock to provide immediate crisis intervention, emotional support, and information to survivors of sexual assault and domestic violence. They also offer support for their families and friends.

I dialed the familiar number dimly lit on the tiny display.

"Crisis Hotline, how may I help you?"

"Hi, this is Diann. I got your page."

"Hi, Diann. There has been a rape, and we need you to respond to the police station. All I know at this point is there is a fourteen-year-old victim with her mother."

"Thanks. I'll be there in thirty minutes."

That was always the dilemma because I lived so far away from the city that it took me a while to respond to the victims. I felt horrible about it. You could say I didn't always obey the speed limits while on call.

As I entered the stale-smelling, pint-size room in the police station being used for interviews, I spotted the young girl with her face in her hands, trembling. My heart ached for her immediately.

I walked up to her and said, "Hi, I'm Diann from the Women's Resource Center and am here to be with you if you have any questions, get anything you may need, and be your support system. I'm sorry it took me so long to get here."

"Diann, we are just finishing up here with the police report. Can you explain to Mary what will happen at the hospital if she decides to get an exam?" asked the detective.

"Mary, first of all, I'm so sorry you are here and going through this. I want you to know this isn't your fault, and we are here for you. You are very brave to be here talking to the police. You are doing a great job. Do you want anything? A soda?"

Mary nodded her head. I went to the vending

machine and got her a Coke. I returned and sat down beside her on the metal chair provided at the round wooden table. The detective was finished with her report.

"There will be what they call a forensic nurse in a special room designed just for rape victims at the hospital, and they conduct special physical exams where they may collect samples of what may be on your body. It's called a PERK exam. Would it make it easier for you if I described what the PERK exam is? Maybe that would make you feel a little calmer? Not knowing something you will go through can be scary," I said to the scared young girl. She was a small-built young lady with blonde curly hair and gorgeous blue eyes.

"Yes, please," she responded with her head held low while wiping a tear from her eye.

"A PERK exam is also called the Physical Evidence Recovery Kit. It is a special medical exam given to people who have been raped and who may want to report the assault to the police, which you are doing now. And I am so proud of you. The exam is different from a regular doctor's exam. This one is done to get evidence of the assault. If the person wants to report it to the police, which you so bravely are doing, the evidence from the kit will help in the investigation and trial of the bad guy for the assault. The exam has to be done within seventy-two hours of the assault. The exam is done at the hospital in the emergency room, by specially trained nurses and asking for it to be done." I informed her while reaching out to take her hand and gave her a sympathetic squeeze.

"Okay, that's what it is, but what do they do during the exam?" Mary asked hesitantly.

"You will be dressed in a gown, and the nurse will first ask you some questions. The nurse then will spread a thin sheet on the floor, and you will be asked to step on it. She will then comb through your hair. This is to see if there is any evidence in your hair. If there is, it will fall onto the sheet. She will turn on a black light, shine it all over your body to see if there is any evidence of bite marks, fluids, and things like that. If there is, she can take samples. She might do an internal exam. If you've had an annual female exam before, it's like that. Any evidence found, the sheet, and the forms you had signed, she'll place it all in the PERK kit box. The kit then goes into a specially designed manila brown envelope. This envelope is then given to the detective doing the investigation. Does this help you understand what will happen during the exam? I know it's a lot to take in."

"Yes, it does, and it makes me less scared," Mary replied.

"Good because it's the smart thing to do in case there is any evidence on your body. It can help prove what happened and who did it."

After speaking with her for a few minutes, she

agreed to the exam. I drove to the hospital and waited in the emergency room. Finally, after about an hour, she walked into the emergency room with her mother. I was beginning to think she had changed her mind, as the hospital was only ten minutes away. I found out later that mother and daughter were discussing all that was about to happen while sitting in the parking lot of the hospital.

I brought Mary and her mother to the forensic room, where I had been many times before. We knocked on the door, and the forensic nurse opened it with a friendly smile. I introduced Mary and her mother to the nurse. We sat down in the chairs provided in the small room, filled with flowered pictures covering the white walls. The nurse then explained to Mary what I had described to her at the police station.

Mary had her exam. It was difficult for her, but with the help of her mother's tender words and me by her side, she came through like a champ. As I sat supporting her, I remembered my own rape. I was being triggered. But I had to stay strong for Mary.

Domestic Violence

It was Friday evening, and Joe and I were watching the eleven o'clock news. I was exhausted after my long week at work. I was on call for the week and had already had one call out the night before with a sexual assault of a two-year-old little girl. I had only gotten three hours of sleep the night before. My pager made that familiar sound once again.

I dialed the number lit on the small display screen and called the hotline number and was informed there was a woman involved in a domestic violence dispute and was at the police station filing a report. I informed the worker that I would be there as soon as possible.

As I drove the familiar route to the PD, my heart raced with a feeling of sadness for a woman I haven't even met. I pulled into the station twenty minutes later. Record time.

I was introduced to Stephanie, a thirty-five-year-old woman with short brown wavy hair and dark brown eyes. She was dressed in a torn light blue, short-sleeved shirt, jeans, and white sneakers. A bruise covered one eye, and she had red scratches with dried blood on her exposed left arm.

"Hi, Stephanie. I'm Diann from The Women's Resource Center, and I'm here as an advocate and to provide you with information regarding domestic violence. I'm here to offer you emotional support, victims' rights information, help in finding needed resources, and assistance in filling out crime victim-related forms. I can also accompany you through the criminal justice proceedings if you wish."

"Thank you, I appreciate that," Stephanie replied.

Once Stephanie finished with her police report, the detective and I suggested to her she go to the hospital to have her eye and her arm checked. She agreed.

I followed her to the local hospital as the detective drove her. While we were waiting for the doctor to see her, I spoke to Stephanie about the local women's shelter and all the resources available for her.

"Stephanie, you realize this wasn't your fault? Your husband is to blame, and you deserve to be treated with respect. Do you have a safe place to go tonight?"

"I do not want to go home to my husband," Stephanie informed me through her tears.

"Let's make a plan, Stephanie. Would you like me to call the shelter and let them know that you will be going there tonight once you are finished being seen by the doctor?" Thankfully, she agreed.

After she was discharged, we sat and talked about her circumstances on the bench outside the hospital. She wanted to purge from the night she had experienced. She also expressed to me why she didn't see the signs her husband was abusive before they met and what it will be like the next time she meets someone. We discussed some of the red flags someone may exhibit. I shared with her what I knew professionally and personally.

"It may feel right now as though you're never going to meet someone who doesn't hit you or that you can trust. It may feel as though you'll never have that relationship where you can do what you want and not have someone question your every move. It may feel as though you're never going to meet that person who makes you feel so special and then treats you like dirt. That person who is not Dr. Jekyll and Mr. Hyde. I am living proof there are people out there that don't treat you like that. I have met them. I had met them when I wasn't ready. One thing for sure that you have to be ready when meeting the next person—you have to be healthy to enter the next relationship. I wasn't ready when my husband and I got together again. I should have taken the time to heal myself first before getting married. I was lucky that Joe loved me enough to hang in there while I healed. I had a lot of baggage after my relationship with my ex. It was much more baggage than after my uncle raped me and then add my ex-husband's abuse. But put all that baggage together and then get married, phew, that's a lot! Then get married, try and learn a new relationship, that's work in itself. Let alone not being healthy. It's hard entering a new relationship even when someone is healthy."

"When coming out of a domestic violence relationship, it is important to be healthy before getting involved in another relationship. But it's hard. We want someone to care for us. We want someone to love us. We reach out. But the bad guys are right there, ready to grab us. They see us coming. They can see us a mile away. They can see our low self-esteem and they prey on that. We don't see the red flags because we want the relationship too much. We don't want to know the truth. We feel our intuition is wrong. If we were healthy, we'd see the red flags and run! So, it's really important to seek counseling for yourself. And work hard. Be honest and open up. It will take some time before you start to feel better, but you'll get there!"

Stephanie sat quietly and listened. I explained to her the red flags to look out for.

"You should look for the possessiveness and the over controlling in men and how and where you spend your time. He may want to do everything with just the two of you. He may want you to quit other activities that you do without him. He may want you to reduce the amount of time you spend with your family and friends. He may even want you to account for all your time or whereabouts like my ex-husband did with me and frequently checking in to be sure you are where you're supposed to be. Sometimes possessiveness is initially flattering. Receiving several phone calls a day could be perceived as 'he really likes me.' But he's actually checking up on you. It borders on stalking. He could be saying something like, 'I called you and couldn't reach you. I missed you. Where were you?' But by doing this numerous times a day, that's different. Is he obsessive?"

"Another red flag is jealousy. This is an insecurity which makes them a high risk for being very possessive, controlling, and abusive. Does he dislike your family or friends? This tends to make you end up not spending time with them. Lying is another one. If you catch him in even the smallest lie, drop him! Is he nice to you but verbally or physically aggressive to someone else? Acts differently when you are alone than when you are with him? Does he mistreat animals or children? Any predatory man can be extraordinarily charming, witty, and fun to be with, like Jim. They can also appear to be very empathic or understanding about a woman telling him of problems in her past, and some can even cry on demand. Charm or charisma is by no means a certain sign that a guy is going to become abusive, but abusive men as a group are probably far more charming than men who are not going to abuse their girlfriends or wives. Does he tell you how absolutely wonderful you are before he really knows you? That is a red flag."

We sat for a half hour discussing how she was feeling, and I then called a cab for Stephanie to take her to the woman's shelter. Once she was there, she was greeted by staff and was provided with a room and more resources. The shelter was where she was going to call home until she could make further plans.

I found out a few days later that Stephanie had filed a restraining order on her husband. This restraining order was a temporary restraining order and was only good for forty-eight hours. Then she met a with a judge, and she had to plead her case, asking for a permanent restraining order which was good for a year in Virginia. The judge granted this order. Her husband had the right to appear and defend himself at this hearing; however, he did not.

After her husband's arrest, he bonded out. At that time, they gave him a court date to appear for arraignment, which was in thirty days. During the arraignment hearing, her husband pleaded guilty to the charges of domestic violence and was sentenced by the judge, which meant Stephanie was spared going to a trial. Since this was the first offense, the husband was sentenced to time served, was given 150 hours of community service, had to attend psychological counseling and anger management courses, and was placed on probation for three years.

Thankfully, Stephanie took the time she needed at the shelter, moved out of her home, and was now living with one of her girlfriends. A brave survivor indeed.

PART FOUR

❦

MENTAL HEALTH AND THE ROAD TO HEALING

CHAPTER 15

Suicidal Ideation

BACK ON FEBRUARY 14, 2006, I wanted to end my life. Joe was out of town from February 12 through 17 at a training in St. Louis. Talking about my abuse as often as I was and helping victims of abuse was taking its toll on me. It caused many flashbacks of Dick and Jim, and I still felt damaged by Uncle Sal. It all caused my anxiety to rise, and in turn, I was losing sleep and becoming depressed. I had low self-esteem and was still insecure when it came to Joe. I wasn't myself. I was hyperventilating and talked myself into the fact I wasn't good enough for anyone. I felt I had no purpose. I figured the best thing for everyone was for me not to be on this earth. You'd think with all the positive work I was doing in the community, I wouldn't feel this way, but PTSD, low self-esteem, and depression were taking over rational thoughts.

I was missing Joe and figured this was the best

time to do it. He wasn't home and couldn't stop me. I reached into my nightstand and removed all the old medicine bottles I could find. There were old sleeping pills left over from my mom and Kurt's old pills, and I figured if I took all the pills in these bottles, that would do the trick. But there was something I had to do first.

I went downstairs into our office and opened up the phone book. I scanned the pages until I found it. A horse rescue farm in Roanoke. I jotted down the phone number and wrote out instructions to Joe about how to transport our horses.

I went back upstairs to the bedroom. I sat at the edge of the bed, looking at the pills. I emptied them all and piled them up. I picked up a bottle of water, placed numerous pills in my hand, and just then, the phone rang. I waited a moment. *Do I answer it, or do I take the pills?* I cried. I didn't know what to do. I picked up the phone without a word.

"Hi, hon! Happy Valentine's Day!! I love you," my wonderful husband said with glee. I gulped. I didn't know what to say. "Hon, are you there?" he asked.

"I'm here. Happy Valentine's Day to you, too. How's the training going?" That was all I could think of to say to him. Imagine that. I was moments away from taking my life, and I was talking to him as if nothing was about to happen.

"It's okay. Kind of boring, but you know how

these things are. They are always boring. How was your day?" How was I going to answer this question, I thought?

"It was okay. I rode the horses for a while. Did some laundry. I didn't have any speaking engagements today, so it was quiet for me."

"Good! I hope you get some rest tonight. It's late, hon. I'm going to hit the hay, and I'll call you tomorrow. Good night, babe. I love you."

"I love you too, hon. Good night." And with those ending words, I realized he had just saved my life. I put the pills away. I went downstairs and ripped up the note regarding the horses. I cried myself to sleep.

I didn't tell Joe. I didn't call for help. I kept this secret within me for a long time. I went into the Women's Resource Center the next day to give a training session as if nothing had happened the night before. Just like that.

I went on with life, continuing with my presentations, deeply depressed, but I went on with a smile on my face. No one knew the black hole I was living with internally. I desperately wanted to talk about it, but I was ashamed. I always wanted to be that person who could take care of everyone, took on all responsibilities, and did the best anyone could. Yet inside, I was drowning. I was treading water as if I was swimming through a huge tidal wave and couldn't catch my breath.

The one great positive in my life was Kurt, as he was doing great. He had joined a Christian group of students while in college. Kurt had many friends within the group and was doing well. He had received his bachelor's degree in business and was thriving at his job. I was one proud momma.

**

In September 2009, once again, I wanted to end my life. I was at my wit's end with all that was going on in my head, the stress, flashbacks, the pressure at work, the hours I was working, and barely getting any sleep. This was when I realized I needed some help. I had gone to counseling in the past, but this time, I felt I needed more professional help.

I was driving to work one morning and felt extreme agitation. My blood pressure was up. I felt like a failure once again. I felt I was no good. I felt I was useless. The way I felt as a child.

As I was driving, I wanted to drive my car into the mountain ahead of me. When I reached the point where I would need to keep my steering wheel straight to hit the mountain, I turned the wheel to stay on the road. I then immediately drove to Joe's office. He had recently gone back to work after retiring from law enforcement, again, in April. He now worked for Social Services. I parked in the parking lot and called him on his cell phone.

"Hon, can you come out to the parking lot. I need to talk to you about something."

"I'll be right there."

I said with tears rolling down my face, "I need help."

"Hon, what's the matter?" Joe said with fear in his voice and reaching out to me with a hug.

"As I was driving to work, I sped up toward the edge of the mountain and was about to crash into it. I didn't want to stop, but at the last minute, I swung the car to miss it. I think I need to see someone."

"Oh, hon. I'm so sorry. Yes, let's make you an appointment." He immediately called my boss and called in sick for me. I sat in my car crying. Sobbing, in fact.

"Wait here, hon, and I'll be right back. I'm going to get a phone book. Hold on." I sat in the car, waiting for Joe to return. I couldn't believe I told him what had happened, but I was also proud of myself for doing so. I was embarrassed but thankfully was strong enough to tell him.

He returned with the phone book, and we both started looking for a psychiatrist for me to call.

"Hon, be sure you find one that is not in our area. There'd be too much of a chance that one of my clients may go there, and I don't want to run into any of them."

We sat and perused the phone book until we found a doctor far enough away.

I dialed. "Hello? Yes, my name is Diann, and I need an emergency visit, please."

"The soonest we can get you in would be on Wednesday. How is eleven a.m.?"

"I'll take it." I turned to Joe and informed him my appointment was in two days.

"I'm taking the rest of the day off, and we'll go home to relax. I don't want you to be alone."

Joe returned to his office, informed his supervisor he was going to be taking the next two days off from work, returned to his car, and we both drove the thirty minutes home. Once there, we both crawled on the couch together and hugged closely for the afternoon. His touch was what I needed. His support was what I needed. We were mostly quiet for the day, and believe it or not, that was what I needed. I didn't need a lot of questions. He did ask me if there was anything I wanted to talk about and told me he was there for me. I wasn't in the mood to discuss anything with him. I was mentally exhausted.

On Wednesday morning, I ventured out for the forty-five-minute drive to the psychiatrist's office. I was nervous. I had never been to a psychiatrist's office before as a patient, only a psychologist. I had no idea what to expect for myself and my condition. I knew the differences between the two were primarily a psychiatrist could prescribe medications and assign a diagnosis of mental illness to patients.

"Diann, would you come with me, please," asked the doctor. I was impressed the doctor himself called the patient to his office. As I sat down on the black leather couch, it was obvious he didn't spare any expense on his furniture.

"Diann, please tell me why you made this appointment."

It all poured out of me, starting with the first time I wanted to kill myself, all the stresses I had been through, my volunteer work, my job, and the abuse. I ended by telling him what I was about to do the other day while driving.

"Diann, I'd like you to fill out this form for me. It should only take you about ten minutes. Would you do that for me, please?" he asked in a soothing voice.

"Sure. Not a problem." He passed me a four-page questionnaire to circle yes or no for some questions and fill in the blanks for others. Twelve minutes later, I passed it back to the doctor. He took about fifteen minutes to review it then turned to me.

"Diann, with everything you've told me, and the results of your test, it is apparent to me you have bipolar, PTSD, and social anxiety." Whoa. This was a lot to take in.

"What? Bipolar?" Now I'm really labeled, I thought. "I don't like the term I'm hearing. Can you please explain to me what bipolar is?" I asked.

"Of course. Bipolar disorder, with its extreme mood swings from depression to mania, used to be called manic-depressive disorder. Bipolar disorder is very serious and can cause risky behavior, even suicidal tendencies. It can be treated with therapy and medication."

"Will I have to take medication?"

"I believe it will benefit you greatly, Diann. I will start you with Seroquel, and let's see how that helps you. We will start slowly at first and go from there. Do you have a counselor you can go to, as well? A combination of medications along with talk therapy is best."

"No, I don't. I will look into it. Thank you."

"I want you to know the symptoms of bipolar depression, which is part of what you have. They are depressed mood with low self-esteem, excessive crying spells, low energy levels and an apathetic view on life, sadness, loneliness, helplessness, feelings of guilt, slow speech, fatigue, poor coordination and concentration, insomnia or oversleeping, thoughts of suicide or dying, changes in appetite, overeating/not eating, unexplainable body aches and pains, lack of interest or pleasure in usual activities. How many of these symptoms do you feel, Diann?"

"Wow. Most of them," I responded.

"That's what I thought," he replied. "As you responded on the form you filled out, I feel you also experience symptoms of bipolar mania. Those symptoms are euphoria or irritability, excessive talking, racing thoughts, inflated self-esteem, unusual energy, less need for sleep, impulsiveness, a reckless pursuit of gratification—shopping sprees, impetuous travel, more and sometimes promiscuous sex, high-risk business investments, fast driving, hallucinations and or delusions, such as psychotic features such as these may be involved in about one out of every two of cases of bipolar mania. Do you recognize some of these?"

"Oh, I sure do. This is a lot to take in. It really upsets me."

"Please try not to let it upset you. It isn't your fault you have bipolar. There's nothing you could have done to prevent it. I also want you to know there is no cure for bipolar. We can help you with medications to help stabilize your mood swings. With medications and help from your counselor, you will begin to feel better. It's all up to you to work with us, Diann."

"Doc, I don't understand why I have social anxiety. I always want attention and feel I am quite social. Can you help me understand this diagnosis, please?"

"Social anxiety disorder, is also called social phobia, is an anxiety disorder in which a person has an excessive and unreasonable fear of social situations. Anxiety—intense nervousness—and self-consciousness arise from a fear of being closely watched, judged, and criticized by others. A person with social anxiety disorder is afraid that he or she will make mistakes, look bad, and be embarrassed or humiliated in front of others."

"A lot of that makes sense to me. I'm constantly looking behind my back for my ex following me. Which I realize is ridiculous, but I can't help it. I can't even go into the grocery store without thinking there may be someone there to hurt me. It's really weird. I suppose I've had this for many years, as I'm always worried about making mistakes and looking bad. I've had that since I was a child with my father. Still, to this day, I feel this way with him," I said with a laugh. "I appreciate your help. I will do my best to help myself."

I left the office in disbelief and a bit confused. I couldn't believe my ears—I was diagnosed with three distinct mental illnesses. I knew about the PTSD from a prior diagnosis, but the other two, these were new to me.

The doctor started me on medications, but within a few weeks, I was sluggish. After going back to my next appointment, the doctor lowered my dosage.

I still wasn't feeling myself. I didn't have the energy I once had. My job required me to have a lot of energy and stamina, as being on call, I often had to go out in the middle of the night. Taking these medications slowed me down, made me lethargic, and they just didn't provide me the energy to complete my job well.

I then made a foolish and critical decision. I stopped taking my medications and stopped going to the doctor. This is something that no one, no one who has bipolar or has any type of mental illness and is on medications should ever do.

I gave a presentation in the fall at the local university. The topic, sexual assault. This was the defining moment, the beginning of the end of my employment at the Women's Resource Center.

My presentation itself was fine, but once the presentation was over, many questions came from students in attendance. My social anxiety had kicked in, and answering their questions became a real struggle. I had recently gone off my meds, hadn't slept well, and felt stressed. Honestly, I shouldn't have even given the presentation. I should have asked my supervisor to take over for me, but that would mean I was a failure in my mind, so I chose not to do the right thing.

They filed a complaint with my employer regarding the question-and-answer time with the students. This was the first time I had ever had a complaint. My supervisor called me into her office and told me about the complaint.

"Diann, I received a call about the presentation you gave at the university. The complaint said, although your presentation was fine, the question-and-answer period wasn't. They said that when questions started being asked, you were short with your answers, dashed through them, giving the questioners the impression you were indifferent to them," she stated.

"I'm sorry they perceived me that way. It wasn't my intention. I just wasn't feeling very well yesterday. I know this doesn't excuse what happened. I should just have called out and not given the presentation. It won't happen again," I replied.

We spoke about it for a few more minutes, concluding this was a onetime deal and to be more careful in the future. I was hurt. No one had ever complained about my work. I had always had great reviews and positive comments. I had conducted hundreds of presentations. Going forward, this incident truly affected my daily routine. It was always on my mind every day. It was distracting.

I put a lot of thought into this on Monday morning, concluding that after all these years, everything that I had been through, the strength and determination, why was I going to let one person's phone call change me? Unfortunately, it did change me. It depressed me.

With the situation at the university on my mind, having stopped my medications and my schedule being as crazy as it was, I was a mess. A few weeks later, my supervisor had been noticing something was up with me.

"Diann, is there anything going on with your job you'd like to discuss with me, or anything personal going on you'd like to share? I've noticed something different about you, and I'd like to help if I could," asked my supervisor.

"No, nothing at all. I can't think of anything." I lied, of course, because that was my habit of not sharing my feelings. I felt that work was not a place for me to be sharing my personal situations. I then left my supervisor's office and went back to my office, feeling sullen.

After the Christmas holiday and after it was my shift to be on call, my supervisor and I had another conversation. This conversation led to a lengthy and loud argument.

"Diann, I know there is something up with you. You haven't been the same since the situation with the university," exclaimed my supervisor that Friday afternoon.

"Okay, honestly, there is. Since that incident at the university, I feel I'm being watched with everything I do. I don't feel I deserved it. There have never been any other instances to warrant me being watched like a hawk. I have worked here for three years, two at this position, and that was my first complaint. Granted, I didn't do well that day, but that was the only time I failed. Believe me, I hate myself for it!" I behaved horribly. Yes, my mental illness was ruining my work environment.

My supervisor raised her voice. "It is my job to make sure you are doing your job well. I agree with you. You have always done a good job. I have no idea what happened that day at the university, but it shouldn't have. It was embarrassing to me to receive a call from them with the information. Those things just can't happen. Yes, I've been in your other presentations to be sure it was a onetime thing, and your other presentations have been just fine."

I blew my top. I didn't appreciate her tone, and my blood pressure was up. I believe my bipolar was kicking in, and I was about to say things I didn't want to say. I ran out of the room like a child. I felt trapped.

I went straight to the director's office to discuss what was occurring with my supervisor and my position. We both agreed that I shouldn't work there anymore. It probably was for the best for my emotional state.

I loved my job; however, it was time for me to take a break and not be in the work environment I was accustomed to. Being around all of the repercussions of violence day in and day out had become too much for me. I, of course, felt like a failure, and yet I shouldn't, but one of the best things that I could've done was not work there anymore, but I didn't feel that way.

CHAPTER 16

Depression

I NOW USED THIS freedom at home to spend more time with the horses. My days at the barn would consist of brushing the horses, cleaning the stalls, and just good horse time. Other days, I would ride and try to enjoy the outside weather. These times didn't last long. You would think that would be excellent therapy for me.

It didn't take long before I became increasingly depressed. There would be days I didn't want to get out of bed. I didn't want to change my clothes, brush my teeth, or do laundry. No self-care at all. It was surprising I even took care of the horses and dogs. I couldn't sleep.

My husband's and my relationship was becoming strained once again. My mood swings in full bloom. I felt Jim was looking into the windows again. Something had to be done. I was almost at a point in my life where I wanted to pack my bags and run. Run from what? I didn't know; I just felt that I needed to run from myself. I was scared. I was lonely. I called my friend Robin, who lives in Maine, and asked her if I could come and live with her for a while.

"Diann, of course, you can. Anytime. What's going on?" replied Robin.

"Robin, I don't know. Joe has done nothing wrong. I just feel trapped. My depression is out of control, and I feel I need a bit of change in scenery and thinking that may help. I'm at a loss of what to do."

I never went to Robin's house.

Joe and I started counseling together again in September 2009, which was before I left WRC. The counselor we chose was a fantastic, knowledgeable man, listened to us, and offered us brilliant advice. He was not too soft on us, as he will call the shots when he sees fit. Which aggravated the hell out of me in the beginning! I just didn't always have the patience for counseling. I knew it was the best thing for me to be doing for my depression, lack of self-esteem, and thoughts of suicide, once again.

For a while, I didn't think the counseling was working because I hadn't started feeling any better. Little did I know at that time, it takes a while, a long, arduous while, for counseling to work. It takes many appointments, hard work, and total commitment. I wanted to feel better, *now*! I wanted the demons inside of me to stop. I continued my counseling with angst.

This time, I made myself a promise that when I found the correct meds, I was going to definitely stay on them. Whatever it took to not be depressed anymore. It is horrible to feel like your life isn't worth living, that those around you couldn't give a shit, even though you know a part of you is only feeling it for a short while, and you are hopeful you were wrong. It's not true, but at that moment, you feel you are so right. It's scary. I didn't want to feel this way any longer.

Thirty-one years since Uncle Sal raped me. That's long enough for him to be controlling me. I'm tired of the thoughts of Dick's and Jim's fists on my face. I'm tired of feeling as though they still are going to make me do things I don't want to do. I need to start living. I have been extending myself for others for so long, and as selfish as it feels, I would like to find some peace within myself for the years I have left on this earth to enjoy for me.

Finally, I mentioned to my counselor that a few years earlier, I was diagnosed with bipolar. He wasn't surprised. Together we discussed going to a doctor immediately and get back on medications. I was willing to do so and made an appointment the following day.

I met with my nurse practitioner at the request of my counselor. Not only was she my NP, I knew her as one of the forensic nurses at the hospital I had responded to for sexual assaults when I worked at WRC. She was at many of those calls, and we worked together.

God willing, soon I would start feeling better. It'd been a long journey.

As anyone with a mental illness knows, it takes time for medications to work and sometimes the medication(s) you start with is not the one you end up with; you can have many changes to your meds. It can get frustrating.

In 2011, my thoughts were clearer, and I felt better. It feels as if my depression had ebbed once again. I'd been home a little over a year, and now I was bored. I found a listing for an administrative position at the local university, and I applied. After two weeks, I was hired and started work at the counseling center, where I answered phones, checked in students, and performed other administrative duties. I settled in and got along well with my coworkers and the counselors.

It wasn't a demanding job, but it was exactly what I needed; to get out of the house and be among people. It was slow at times, so I would ask my supervisor if there was something more for me to do. They were few and far between, these times when she would have something for me, but it elated me when she would hand me a separate project to work on. They knew me for getting things done quickly.

Little did I know, my mania had kicked in. I loved it when the mania came. I could get so much done in a short period. The only downfall to mania was it lasted for such a short period of time, then I would crash. I crashed hard, and my depression would grow and settle in. My mind was scrambling a bit to keep up with itself, as ideas were coming so fast that they intersected one another at every conceivable angle. The more I tried to slow down my thinking, the more I became aware I couldn't. My enthusiasms were going into overdrive as well, although there was often some underlying thread of logic in what I was doing. I hid it well, wearing my mask, a mask I perfected through the years. No one ever knew how low I sank. I didn't show it to the public, my coworkers, and especially Joe. Sometimes for comfort, at lunchtime, I would go to McDonald's, then I would go to the drugstore, pick up an enormous bag of M&M's, put it in my desk, and munch on them all day. The next day the bag would be empty. Between the meds and all the junk food I ate, I gained sixty pounds.

As time went on, my depression was surfacing again. I would start feeling that a breakdown was about to happen. I didn't want to do it in the office, nor have anyone see me. It wasn't out of the ordinary for me to ask for a break during these occurrences. I took these regularly, at least a few times a week, and I think that led some to think I was a heavy smoker. I'd go outside, gathering myself back up for fifteen minutes, then return to my desk. Those breaks would help only on a temporary basis. I was also calling out sick at least once or twice a month.

I started seeing my original psychiatrist again. On my next visit with him, I told him of my mania and how I would then crash, so then he would change my medication and possibly change the dose of another medication.

For about a month or two, the new cocktail of meds and dosages would help. Then its effects would wane. I'd go back to my psychiatrist, and it would be time for a change once again. This continual challenge that went on month after month for a few years was frustrating. But I would not stop taking my meds. This time, I was determined to stick with it. Oh, I'm not saying I didn't think about giving up my meds, I did. But in my heart, I knew we'd find a solution, and I wanted to feel better, so I continued working hard with my meds and my counselor. The mix of the two was working well, then they weren't. Bipolar is a hard illness to live with.

I still enjoyed working and seeing the students regularly. Some would come in sad for a particular reason, and I would empathize with them while checking them in at the desk.

Typically, they looked up at me with a slight smile. I always tried to brighten up their day, even if it was just with a return of a smile. Some students made small talk with me, and I enjoyed the commentary. However, I continued to go out for breaks a few times a day, specifically for the possible breakdowns. I worked like this for another year and a half.

***

It was March 2013 when I felt the need to walk out of the office and go directly to my family physician. I told my supervisor I was leaving to go to the doctor. She knew I didn't have an appointment.

I saw Cris, my nurse practitioner, as an emergency appointment.

"Cris, I'm not sure how or if I'm going to make it some days. I take breaks at the office regularly because I think I'm going to have a breakdown. I can't keep doing this. What can I do? I'm already on a lot of medications. Why do I feel this way?"

"Diann, you are stressed and depressed. Are you getting any sleep?"

"Not enough."

"Okay, I'm going to write you a note that you don't have to go back to work for two weeks. I want you to concentrate on sleeping and resting. I also want you to contact your psychiatrist and tell him about today's appointment."

"Thanks, Cris. I will call him as soon as I get home. I'll stop at my office and give this note to my supervisor."

After I left Cris's office, I went directly to my supervisor. Behind closed doors, I handed her the note.

As I left the office, I walked with my head hung low. I didn't want to tell my supervisor or anyone else the reason I wouldn't be in the office for two weeks.

It wasn't anyone else's business, and it embarrassed me.

During my two-week reprieve, all I wanted to do was feel the comfort of my sheets and pillow. I would get up to feed the dogs and take care of the horses, and occasionally I would sit on the couch and get on my laptop. But mostly stayed in bed. Just before I knew it was time for Joe to come home, I would jump in the shower to look presentable for him so he wouldn't know I had been in bed all day, even though I was prescribed rest. He would know nothing. He didn't have a clue.

"Hon, how was your day?" I would ask him when he returned home from work.

"I had a few fraud arrests, but nothing major. What did you do today?"

"I was with the horses for a while, played with the dogs, cleaned the house, did some laundry, and watched my soap operas." As I lied to him, I could feel a knot in my stomach. I knew he wouldn't notice if I had cleaned the house or did laundry, so that was a good lie. I didn't want him knowing I was in bed most of the day. Since I looked refreshed from my shower, he had no reason to believe anything was wrong.

"Hon, you are to be resting. Please take it easy tomorrow, okay?"

Each day was the same. I never felt like getting out of bed. I went to my counseling appointments that week. I explained to my counselor what I was going through, and he told me my depression was taking over. No duh, I thought.

"I want you to obey doctor's orders and continue to bed rest. It doesn't matter that Joe knows. I'm sure he wants you better," said my counselor.

"I agree he wants me better, but I just feel ashamed to be in bed all day. It isn't like me to not do anything. I don't want to be *different* in his eyes," I replied.

"Diann, you are already different in his eyes by the way you've been acting. If he sees you taking care of yourself, he will feel good about that, and I know he will support you."

By the end of the second week, I knew I wasn't ready to go back to work. I called my psychiatrist's office for a quick appointment.

"As you know, I've just had two weeks off from work. I'm not ready to go back to work. I'm still really depressed and don't feel I can face up to anything right now."

"Okay, Diann. I will write you up a note to give you a month off. Do you think that will help?"

"I do, and thank you."

When I arrived home, I faxed the note the doctor had given me to my supervisor. I didn't even have the decency to call her. I was embarrassed by this. I know now I shouldn't have been, but I was.

At the end of the month, once again, I wasn't ready to go back to work, and my psychiatrist wrote a note giving me three months off of work. He also suggested we change one of my medications.

I called my supervisor this time and informed her of the doctor's decision.

"I'm sorry I am leaving you guys on a ledge like this. I know it's putting you with extra work without me there. I apologize."

"Diann, no need to apologize. We just want you to get better."

As I was continuing my counseling sessions and appointments with my doctors, I didn't feel much change in how I felt. I was becoming anxious to feel better. I told both my doctors I might as well not even be on meds if my body would not accept these meds and change the way I felt. They told me I needed to continue to work hard in my counseling sessions and give the meds a chance to work. Typically, new meds take about a month to work.

In the meantime, I was still alone all day long while Joe was at work. I was having hallucinations that Jim was peeking in my windows. I couldn't go into stores alone. I feared someone was going to shoot people because of the shooting on campus that happened a few months prior. If Joe went to the store with me, I felt better. I was still on edge that something bad was going to happen.

While shopping, I also felt claustrophobic. If the store was too crowded, I would start having panic attacks and had to leave. I couldn't handle it. Joe and

I would figure out times of the day when stores would be less crowded in order for me to enter. It was a hell of a way to live.

**

In August, my son was getting married. This was supposed to be an exciting time in my life. It was, don't get me wrong, but my mental health held me back. My depression was still getting the best of me. I probably should have been more involved, but my mind wouldn't allow it. I put on a good show, carrying a smile that hid my pain. I certainly didn't want Kurt, my little boy, to think anything was wrong on his special day.

The reception was packed with over 100 people, which made my anxiety rise and caused me to take many breaks by going outside. I felt rude for not going through the ballroom to introduce myself as the groom's mother, but I couldn't do it. I felt much safer sitting at our table ahead of the pack, facing the groom and bride's table.

When it was time for the bride and groom to leave, I was outside and almost missed it. As I was heading back to the reception hall, I could see everyone lined up outside throwing rice. At the last minute, I caught a glimpse of Kurt, and I ran to kiss him. My heart would have been broken if I wasn't able to say goodbye. It was a beautiful sight to see. My son had become such a wonderful young man. Married. Kurt, my baby, the one with whom I had gone through so much, was no longer a baby. I tried to hide my tears but to no avail. They came rushing down my cheeks.

Kurt had chosen the best woman in the world to marry. Anna was a sweet, beautiful, loving, Christian woman who I knew would take great care of my son and love him with all her heart. She was perfect. She came from a large, loving family, and I knew my son had wonderful in-laws. I couldn't have asked for a better woman for my son to marry.

My medications continued to change almost every two months, as their effectiveness was sporadic. I stayed on one or two medications, and then the doctor would make the dosage higher but remove one medication and replace it with another. I felt like a research project. It was disheartening to try so many meds only to find they didn't work. This only added to my depression. My life with medications continued this way for another five years. I continued working adamantly in counseling, having sessions once a month.

CHAPTER 17

Living for Today

THROUGHOUT THE YEARS, JOE and I had often tried to locate my sister Cynthia, the daughter my mother lost in the court system many years ago, but to no avail. In July 2020, I used the availability of Facebook to locate her by searching the adopted last name I believed Cindi gained when she was six. I found a group called Search Squad which conducts searches for missing persons, whether it be through adoptions or other means. I listed as much information as I knew about her. Two hours later, they had located my sister!

I sent Cindi a Facebook friend request, and within a few moments, she responded with a private message. And with that, we messaged for over an hour. I was overwhelmed with emotion. Joy and happy tears. All these years of searching, over. I had found her. My sister was on the other end of my laptop. Finally.

I called my brother Stephen the following day.

He was ecstatic as he remembered her when he was seven and was in court with her the day she was adopted. The day my mother lost her. I was delighted to be able to provide this happiness and closure for him. The three of us were able to be together before he passed away in September.

Cindi and I keep in touch via Facebook and the telephone, getting to know one another. I always felt as if something was missing without knowing where she was, and now I feel complete with Cindi in my life. She is such a blessing.

Watching my grandchildren grow up is one of the highlights of my life. My son has provided me many proud moments. He received his master's degree, has a terrific job, married a wonderful woman, and has three beautiful children. I couldn't be more proud he is my son.

My relationship with Joe is healthy, and we haven't been happier in all the twenty-three years we have been married. We are two imperfect people who refuse to give up on one another. I am truly blessed to have found him and thankful for that day his brother introduced me to him! He continues to support me in all endeavors. I notice how he may try to prevent me from having any triggers from my past abuse. Such as if there is a song on the radio that had triggered me in the past. The days when Uncle Sal and I played pool and the radio was on, some songs stuck in my head. When those songs come on, he is quick to turn them off. Now, I turn it back on. I have worked through the triggers and am proud I am past them. If there is a domestic violence case reported on the news, in the past, Joe would have changed the channel to prevent me from watching it. Now, we can watch it and discuss it. What used to be my reaction to triggers are now just memories. I no longer feel the physical reactions to them—the stomach aches, headaches or the panic attacks. Now, it's just an observance.

I don't have any feelings of jealousy, as I now have self-esteem, a much better self-image, and I trust Joe with all my heart. Joe going to counseling with me those years certainly helped me work out my issues of the possibility that he didn't love me enough. I had set unrealistic expectations in our marriage, and the two of us attending counseling made me realize what damage I was doing. My past experiences with Dick and Jim were interfering with the relationship with Joe. All of these past abusive behaviors from Uncle Sal, Dick, and Jim used to be a daily reminder. Now that I have healed, I remember how I felt, but those feelings no longer control me. Even the relationship, or lack thereof, with my father was damaging.

I can attest to how important counseling has been for me. And I can also say our counselor was one of the best. I know he would say that my hard work is what caused my healing, but without his guidance, I wouldn't be where I am today.

If you ever feel you are not comfortable with your

counselor, find another one. There are plenty of good counselors available. You may not find the right one the first time, and there is nothing wrong with changing. It may even take a few times. Please don't let that be the reason why you don't go to counseling.

It's wonderful to be in a relationship where it feels safe to be who I want to be. I don't have to worry about doing what I want to do, what friends I want to spend time with, going to the store and not worrying about how much time I spend, and if I don't want to do chores one day, I don't have to, nor do I have to worry if I do them perfectly!

I have learned that when you go to counseling, be honest and upfront with how you are feeling in your sessions. It took me months to be honest with my counselor about my bipolar diagnosis. If I had told him when I knew of the diagnosis, I could have been on the road to recovery that much sooner.

Being honest in counseling about your abuse is important. Becoming a survivor of abuse won't happen overnight. It takes time. Be patient. The more you express yourself, the sooner you will heal.

Please never give up when you are given medications from a psychiatrist. Please don't decide to stop taking your medications. Always let the doctor know exactly how you're feeling. They may change the medication or the dosage to fit what is best for you. It takes time, but eventually, it works, as it did for me. It can become depressing, feeling like it isn't working. But by giving it time, you will be on the road to recovery.

My psychiatrist has found the right mix of three medications, and I have stayed on them for three years. With the number of years of counseling I had put in, my anxiety is at bay, and I'm not depressed. I have also lost forty of those sixty pounds. I have found that it's important to have the right amount of sleep and take my medications. All of which keeps me on track. It has been a lot of work, but worth it. I'm thankful I didn't give up. I will have to be on medications for the rest of my life, as bipolar is a condition that is not something that goes away, but it is a condition that can be controlled. I have moved away from the stigma of mental illness and am not ashamed.

I have been polishing my presentations for domestic violence. I am looking forward to speaking in the community once again. I don't ever want to give up the opportunity to use my voice to help survivors of abuse.

EPILOGUE

I FEEL IT WOULD HAVE made an enormous difference in my life if my parents would have helped me after my rape, hence my mental stability. I wouldn't have felt it was my fault, and I wouldn't have tried to find love in all the wrong places. I'm not sure if I would have started drinking at fourteen and many other crazy things I did in my life. However, because they didn't help, it led me to the path of helping others. I wouldn't trade that in a million years. I have forgiven them. I understand they raised me the best way they knew how at the time.

Do I wish I had communicated better with my parents throughout my life? Certainly. For anyone reading this book, if you don't have a good relationship with your parents or your children, please do the best you can to resolve your differences. Life is too short. You probably have more than you realize to talk about, and it will only help you both in the long run. Make that phone call. Not everyone is reciprocal, but at least you can make that first step. They will know you are there when they are ready.

Having been a victim of sexual assault and domestic violence, it took time to become a survivor. Remember, none of it was your fault. Do not give up. It took me a long time in counseling and the support of my loving husband to proudly say I'm a survivor.

Working at the Women's Resource Center also showed me that there are people in the world that care about SA and DV victims. It was wonderful to surround myself with such individuals. Those I worked with, I will be forever grateful. They do not realize the impact they made in my life.

The first time I told my personal story of abuse in public was the hardest. It was the scariest time. I was afraid that my abuser was in the audience. I was still living in the same state and was afraid he would be in the audience. I still continued. I wanted people to hear my story in case they needed help. That is what I still want today. It truly gives others empowerment. It may help them leave their situation, have victims feel they are not alone, give validation to many, and help individuals understand what people may have been going through.

When I learned I had bipolar, I did a lot of reading on the topic. Some interesting information I found is after a child-victim of sexual assault, when the family is supportive, gets immediate help for the child, and avoids any blaming or stigmatization, the long-term effects can be lessened. However, when the family does not understand, blames the child for the sexual abuse or cannot accept that the child was victimized, the impact can be truly devastating because the family's reaction confirms the child's worst fears: that s/he did something wrong or did not do enough to prevent the sexual abuse.

In these cases, the family members become coconspirators in the abuse because, in failing to give the child what s/he needs during a time of tragedy, they may do far more damage to the child than the abuser did. It is no surprise that children will feel stigmatized by the sexual abuse if their families treat them with disdain and disgust. And, in turn, can lead to bipolar, depression, etc. These readings were also validating. Much of my work was validating to me.

Bipolar is awful beyond words when not treated properly. It bleeds relationships through suspicion; lack of confidence and self-respect, the inability to enjoy life, to talk or think normally, the exhaustion, the night terrors, and the day terrors. Others think they know what it is like to be depressed because they have gone through a divorce, lost a job, or broken up with someone. But these experiences carry with them feelings. Depression is tiresome. People cannot stand being around you when you are depressed.

I hope this book has helped many people, including my family. They may think or thought they knew me. I can tell them right now, they had no idea who I was and who I am today. I am hopeful this book has enlightened them to some extent. No one will ever know the pain I have endured, nor the strength it has taken to come to where I am today. That is okay; what I hope is they would understand and hopefully forgive me for anything I may have done or said that hurt them. I hurt many people on the way to calling myself a survivor. For that, I am deeply sorry, and hopefully, in time, they will or have already forgiven me. The abuse I endured wasn't my fault. The pain I inflicted on others because of what I went through was.

I realized what I was searching for was within me all along. True forgiveness of myself. After all, my unhealthy relationships led to my son being abused. But I had to make that forgiveness happen; no one else could do it for me. Always searching for answers and apologies for my past traumas and answers to why some parents do not support their children after they are abused. After finding some answers, I could move on with my life.

The worthlessness I learned as a child stayed with me as an adult. The sum of all my experiences conditioned me to believe that violence in relationships was acceptable—all people interacted this way; violence was a fact in a relationship, not the exception.

And for all I have lived, I am proud. I've made significant progress in these years. I am excited to see where my next journey brings me in life.

I have taken "stifle it" and turned it into "speak

it" because everyone has a right to a voice.

Cheers! To life!

Life's Greatest Sorrow CAN BE Your Greatest Purpose!

ACKNOWLEDGMENTS

Thank you to those who believed in me to use my voice to help others, to teach children, and be a support system to many survivors of abuse.

Thank you to my editor, Kerry Dill Genova, for her incredible wisdom, willingness to work with me and to pour insights into the growth of this book.

Thank you to Detective Mangini, who handled my son's abuse case professionally and treated my son with care and the Coral Springs Police Department, who went above and beyond the call of duty for me each and every time I needed them.

Thank you to my friend, Polly Currier, who provided me endless hours of support, not only throughout the years but also during the process of writing this book.

Thank you to my son, Kurt, who was the impetus for my helping victims of child abuse and domestic violence. Together we made a difference. 143

And thank you to my husband for his unwavering support and love. You've been a God-given sounding board, soul mate, and best friend. Without you, this book would not exist.

THANK YOU

Dear Reader,

Thank you so much for supporting me by reading my book. I can't even begin to tell you how much it means to me. I am independently published, so I rely on readers like you to spread the word of my book.

One way to help spread the word, if you enjoyed my book, would be to leave a review on Amazon. Having that recognition from you would be deeply appreciated.

Please follow me on Facebook, as I would love to hear from you!

Facebook:
https://www.facebook.com/diannfurbushdiaz - Author Diann Diaz

You can also visit my webpage for further information for my upcoming book, *"Domestic Violence Victims – Why Do They Stay."*

Website: www.dianndiaz.com

Email: dianndiaz@gmail.com

TRAININGS

A Forensic look at building Safer Relationships
Basic Advocacy: Sexual Violence
Child & Youth Advocacy
Choose Respect: Healthy Teen Relationships
Community Advocacy and Leadership Development
for Rural SV Providers
Crisis Intervention Volunteer Training
Darkness to Light
Domestic Abuse among Older Adults
Eighth National Conference on Child Sexual Abuse
and Exploitation Prevention
Emerging Issues in Gender-based violence work on
college campuses
Exploring Ethics in the Prevention Field 2020
Forensic Look at Everyday Heroes by Carillion
Corporate University
Mentors in Violence Prevention
Preventing Sexual Harassment
Regional Conference on Domestic Violence
Safe Dates: An adolescent dating abuse prevention
curriculum

Sexual Assault Investigation Techniques
Sexual Violence
Southwest Virginia Domestic Violence Conference
Stop Abuse Advocate Training
Train the Trainer: Health Care Response to Intimate Partner Violence
Train the Trainer: Responding to intimate partner violence in the healthcare setting

PRESENTATIONS of PERSONAL STORY

AMSA Students at Virginia Tech
Citizens Against Family Violence Vigil
Clothesline Project(s)
Domestic Violence Conference at Radford University
Floyd United Methodist Church
For Survivors of Trauma
Healing through Creativity
Pre-Medical Honor Society at Virginia Tech
Remember Victims who have lost their lives to Domestic Violence
Sexual Assault Prevention Rally
Sexual Violence Class at Virginia Tech
Southwest Virginia Legal Aid Society
Southwest Virginia Regional Conference on Domestic Violence – 2007
Southwest Virginia Regional Conference on Domestic Violence – 2008
Virginia Cooperative Extension 4-H Youth

Development at Virginia Tech
Women's Resource Center- Emergency Advocate Trainings (quarterly, 4 years)
Women's Symposium – Radford University

RESOURCES

Break the Cycle: Supporting young people between 12 and 24 to build healthy relationships and create an abuse-free culture. **http:/www.breakthecycle.org/**

DomesticShelters.org: Educational information, hotline, and searchable database of services in your area. Go to website, type in your zip code and an area hotline will appear.
https://www.domesticshelters.org/

Love Is Respect (National Dating Abuse Hotline)
https://www.loveisrespect.org/ 1-866-331-9474

National Child Abuse Hotline 1-800-4-A-Child (1-800-422-4453)
https://www.childhelp.org/childhelp-hotline/

National Domestic Violence Hotline – 1-800-799-7233 (SAFE) or 1-800-787-3244 (TTY) This is anonymous, confidential help available 24/7.
https://www.thehotline.org/

RAINN – to speak with someone who is trained to help, call the **National Sexual Assault Hotline** at 800-656-HOPE (4673) or chat online at **https://hotline.rainn.org/online**
https://www.rainn.org/

Suicide Hotline - If you or someone you know is in crisis, call the Lifeline (USA) at 1-800-273-8255 for 24/7, anonymous, free crisis counseling. **https://suicidepreventionlifeline.org/**

DEFINITIONS

Bipolar

Bipolar disorder (formerly called manic-depressive illness or manic depression) is a mental disorder that causes unusual shifts in mood, energy, activity levels, concentration, and the ability to carry out day-to-day tasks.

There are three types of bipolar disorder. All three types involve clear changes in mood, energy, and activity levels. These moods range from periods of extremely "up," elated, irritable, or energized behavior (known as manic episodes) to very "down," sad, indifferent, or hopeless periods (known as depressive episodes). Less severe manic periods are known as hypomanic episodes.

- Bipolar I Disorder— defined by manic episodes that last at least 7 days, or by manic symptoms that are so severe that the person needs immediate hospital care. Usually, depressive episodes occur as well, typically lasting at least 2 weeks. Episodes of depression with mixed features (having depressive symptoms and manic symptoms at the same time) are also possible.

- Bipolar II Disorder— defined by a pattern of depressive episodes and hypomanic episodes, but not the full-blown manic episodes that are typical of Bipolar I Disorder.
- Cyclothymic Disorder (also called Cyclothymia)— defined by periods of hypomanic symptoms as well as periods of depressive symptoms lasting for at least 2 years (1 year in children and adolescents). However, the symptoms do not meet the diagnostic requirements for a hypomanic episode and a depressive episode.

Sometimes a person might experience symptoms of bipolar disorder that do not match the three categories listed above, which is referred to as "other specified and unspecified bipolar and related disorders."

Bipolar disorder is typically diagnosed during late adolescence (teen years) or early adulthood. Occasionally, bipolar symptoms can appear in children. Bipolar disorder can also first appear during a woman's pregnancy or following childbirth. Although the symptoms may vary over time, bipolar disorder usually requires lifelong treatment. Following a prescribed treatment plan can help people manage their symptoms and improve their quality of life.

Signs and Symptoms

People with bipolar disorder experience periods of unusually intense emotion, changes in sleep patterns and activity levels, and uncharacteristic behaviors—often without recognizing their likely harmful or undesirable effects. These distinct periods are called "mood episodes." Mood episodes are very different from the moods and behaviors that are typical for the person. During an episode, the symptoms last every day for most of the day. Episodes may also last for longer periods, such as several days or weeks.

People having a manic episode may:

- Feel very "up," "high," elated, or irritable or touchy
- Feel "jumpy" or "wired"
- Have a decreased need for sleep
- Have a loss of appetite
- Talk very fast about a lot of different things
- Feel like their thoughts are racing
- Think they can do a lot of things at once
- Do risky things that show poor judgment, such as eat and drink excessively, spend or give

away a lot of money, or have reckless sex

- Feel like they are unusually important, talented, or powerful

People having a depressive episode may:

- Feel very sad, "down," empty, worried, or hopeless
- Feel slowed down or restless
- Have trouble falling asleep, wake up too early, or sleep too much
- Experience increased appetite and weight gain
- Talk very slowly, feel like they have nothing to say, forget a lot
- Have trouble concentrating or making decisions
- Feel unable to do even simple things
- Have little interest in almost all activities, a decreased or absent sex drive, or an inability to experience pleasure ("anhedonia")

Sometimes people experience both manic and depressive symptoms in the same episode. This kind of episode is called an episode with mixed features. People experiencing an episode with mixed features may feel very sad, empty, or hopeless, while, at the same, time feeling extremely energized.

A person may have bipolar disorder even if their

symptoms are less extreme. For example, some people with bipolar disorder (Bipolar II) experience hypomania, a less severe form of mania. During a hypomanic episode, a person may feel very good, be able to get things done, and keep up with day-to-day life. The person may not feel that anything is wrong, but family and friends may recognize the changes in mood or activity levels as possible bipolar disorder. Without proper treatment, people with hypomania can develop severe mania or depression.

Reference:
https://www.nimh.nih.gov/health/topics/bipolar-disorder/

❧

Child Abuse

Every year more than 3 million reports of child abuse are made in the United States.

Child abuse is when a parent or caregiver, whether through action or failing to act, causes injury, death, emotional harm or risk of serious harm to a child. There are many forms of child maltreatment, including neglect, physical abuse, sexual abuse, exploitation and emotional abuse.

Reference: https://www.childhelp.org/child-abuse/

❧

Child sexual abuse

When a perpetrator intentionally harms a minor physically, psychologically, sexually, or by acts of neglect, the crime is known as child abuse. This page focuses specifically on child sexual abuse and the warning signs that this crime may be occurring.

Child sexual abuse is a form of child abuse that includes sexual activity with a minor. A child cannot consent to any form of sexual activity, period. When a perpetrator engages with a child this way, they are committing a crime that can have lasting effects on the victim for years. Child sexual abuse does not need to include physical contact between a perpetrator and a child.

Some forms of child sexual abuse include:

- Exhibitionism, or exposing oneself to a minor
- Fondling
- Intercourse
- Masturbation in the presence of a minor or forcing the minor to masturbate
- Obscene phone calls, text messages, or digital interaction
- Producing, owning, or sharing pornographic images or movies of children
- Sex of any kind with a minor, including vaginal, oral, or anal

- Sex trafficking
- Any other sexual conduct that is harmful to a child's mental, emotional, or physical welfare

What do perpetrators of child sexual abuse look like?

The majority of perpetrators are someone the child or family knows. **As many as 93 percent of victims under the age of 18 know the abuser**. A perpetrator does not have to be an adult to harm a child. They can have any relationship to the child, including an older sibling or playmate, family member, a teacher, a coach or instructor, a caretaker, or the parent of another child. According to **1 in 6**, "[Child] sexual abuse is the result of abusive behavior that takes advantage of a child's vulnerability and is in no way related to the sexual orientation of the abusive person."

Abusers can manipulate victims to stay quiet about the sexual abuse using a number of different tactics. Often an abuser will use their position of power over the victim to coerce or intimidate the child. They might tell the child that the activity is normal or that they enjoyed it. An abuser may make threats if the child refuses to participate or plans to tell another adult. Child sexual abuse is not only a physical violation; it is a violation of trust and/or authority.

How can I protect my child from sexual abuse?

A big part of protecting your child is about creating a dialogue. Read more to learn about creating this dialogue and keeping your child safe.

- Talk to Your Child if You Suspect Sexual Abuse
- Protecting Children from Sexual Abuse

What are the warning signs?

Child sexual abuse isn't always easy to spot. The perpetrator could be someone you've known a long time or trust, which may make it even harder to notice. Consider the following warning signs:

- Physical signs:
- Bleeding, bruises, or swelling in genital area
- Bloody, torn, or stained underclothes
- Difficulty walking or sitting
- Frequent urinary or yeast infections
- Pain, itching, or burning in genital area

Behavioral signs:

- Changes in hygiene, such as refusing to bathe or bathing excessively
- Develops phobias
- Exhibits signs of depression or post-traumatic stress disorder
- Expresses suicidal thoughts, especially in adolescents

- Has trouble in school, such as absences or drops in grades
- Inappropriate sexual knowledge or behaviors
- Nightmares or bed-wetting
- Overly protective and concerned for siblings, or assumes a caretaker role
- Returns to regressive behaviors, such as thumb sucking
- Runs away from home or school
- Self-harms
- Shrinks away or seems threatened by physical contact

Where can I get help?

- If you want to talk to someone anonymously, call the National Child Abuse Hotline at 800.4.A.CHILD (422-4453), any time 24/7.
- Learn more about being an adult survivor of childhood sexual abuse.
- To speak with someone who is trained to help, call the National Sexual Assault Hotline at 800.656.HOPE (4673) or chat online at **online.rainn.org**.

Reference: https://www.childhelp.org/child-abuse/

✍

Depression

Depression (major depressive disorder or clinical depression) is a common but serious mood disorder. It causes severe symptoms that affect how you feel, think, and handle daily activities, such as sleeping, eating, or working. To be diagnosed with depression, the symptoms must be present for at least two weeks.

Signs and Symptoms

If you have been experiencing some of the following signs and symptoms most of the day, nearly every day, for at least two weeks, you may be suffering from depression:

- Persistent sad, anxious, or "empty" mood
- Feelings of hopelessness, or pessimism
- Irritability
- Feelings of guilt, worthlessness, or helplessness
- Loss of interest or pleasure in hobbies and activities
- Decreased energy or fatigue
- Moving or talking more slowly
- Feeling restless or having trouble sitting still
- Difficulty concentrating, remembering, or making decisions

- Difficulty sleeping, early-morning awakening, or oversleeping
- Appetite and/or weight changes
- Thoughts of death or suicide, or suicide attempts
- Aches or pains, headaches, cramps, or digestive problems without a clear physical cause and/or that do not ease even with treatment

Not everyone who is depressed experiences every symptom. Some people experience only a few symptoms while others may experience many. Several persistent symptoms in addition to low mood are required for a diagnosis of major depression, but people with only a few – but distressing – symptoms may benefit from treatment of their "subsyndromal" depression. The severity and frequency of symptoms and how long they last will vary depending on the individual and his or her particular illness. Symptoms may also vary depending on the stage of the illness.

Reference:
https://www.nimh.nih.gov/health/topics/depression/

❧

Domestic Violence

Domestic violence is the willful intimidation, physical

assault, battery, sexual assault, and/or other **abusive behavior** as part of a systematic pattern of power and control perpetrated by one intimate partner against another. It includes physical violence, sexual violence, psychological violence, and emotional abuse. The frequency and severity of domestic violence can vary dramatically; however, the one constant component of domestic violence is one partner's consistent efforts to maintain power and control over the other.

Domestic violence is an epidemic affecting individuals in every community regardless of age, economic status, sexual orientation, gender, race, religion, or nationality. It is often accompanied by emotionally abusive and controlling behavior that is only a fraction of a systematic pattern of dominance and control. Domestic violence can result in physical injury, psychological trauma, and in severe cases, even death. The devastating physical, emotional, and psychological consequences of domestic violence can cross generations and last a lifetime.

It is not always easy to determine in the early stages of a relationship if one person will become abusive. Domestic violence intensifies over time. Abusers may often seem wonderful and perfect initially, but gradually become more aggressive and controlling as the relationship continues.

What Does Abuse Include?

Abuse may begin with behaviors that may easily be

dismissed or downplayed such as name-calling, threats, possessiveness, or distrust. Abusers may apologize profusely for their actions or try to convince the person they are abusing that they do these things out of love or care. However, violence and control always intensifies over time with an abuser, despite the apologies. What may start out as something that was first believed to be harmless (e.g., wanting the victim to spend all their time only with them because they love them so much) escalates into extreme control and abuse (e.g., threatening to kill or hurt the victim or others if they speak to family, friends, etc.). Some examples of abusive tendencies include but are not limited to:

- Telling the victim that they can never do anything right
- Showing jealousy of the victim's family and friends and time spent away
- Accusing the victim of cheating
- Keeping or discouraging the victim from seeing friends or family members
- Embarrassing or shaming the victim with put-downs
- Controlling every penny spent in the household
- Taking the victim's money or refusing to give

them money for expenses

- Looking at or acting in ways that scare the person they are abusing
- Controlling who the victim sees, where they go, or what they do
- Dictating how the victim dresses, wears their hair, etc.
- Stalking the victim or monitoring their victim's every move (in person or also via the internet and/or other devices such as GPS tracking or the victim's phone)
- Preventing the victim from making their own decisions
- Telling the victim that they are a bad parent or threatening to hurt, kill, or take away their children
- Threatening to hurt or kill the victim's friends, loved ones, or pets
- Intimidating the victim with guns, knives, or other weapons
- Pressuring the victim to have sex when they don't want to or to do things sexually they are not comfortable with
- Forcing sex with others
- Refusing to use protection when having sex or

sabotaging birth control

- Pressuring or forcing the victim to use drugs or alcohol
- Preventing the victim from working or attending school, harassing the victim at either, keeping their victim up all night so they perform badly at their job or in school
- Destroying the victim's property

Is Domestic Violence Always Physical Abuse?

It is important to note that domestic violence does not always manifest as physical abuse. Emotional and psychological abuse can often be just as extreme as physical violence. Lack of physical violence does not mean the abuser is any less dangerous to the victim, nor does it mean the victim is any less trapped by the abuse.

What Happens When the Abusive Relationship Ends?

Domestic violence does not always end when the victim escapes the abuser, tries to terminate the relationship, and/or seeks help. Often, it intensifies because the abuser feels a loss of control over the victim. Abusers frequently continue to stalk, harass, threaten, and try to control the victim after the victim escapes. In fact, the victim is often in the most danger directly following the escape of the relationship or when they seek help: 1/5 of homicide victims with restraining orders are murdered within two days of obtaining the order; 1/3 are murdered within the first month.

Unfair blame is frequently put upon the victim of abuse because of assumptions that victims choose to stay in abusive relationships. The truth is, bringing an end to abuse is not a matter of the victim choosing to leave; it is a matter of the victim being able to safely *escape* their abuser, the abuser choosing to stop the abuse, or others (e.g., law enforcement, courts) holding the abuser accountable for the abuse they inflict.

For anonymous, confidential help available 24/7, call the National Domestic Violence Hotline at 1-800-799-7233 (SAFE) or 1-800-787-3224 (TTY) now.

Reference: https://ncadv.org/learn-more

❧

Emotional Abuse

It's a common and damaging myth – without bruises, cuts, and broken bones, bandages or a black eye, it's not *really* abuse. Yet being controlled, feeling scared or being forcefully isolated are just some of the markers of emotional abuse, a very real and prevalent type of intimate partner violence

Emotional abusers prey on a victim's self-esteem and emotional abuse is often a precursor to physical abuse. But, emotional abuse can also exist on its own, meaning you may be abused and never have a visible injury to show for it.

To identify if what you're experiencing is emotional abuse, ask yourself the following questions:

Does your partner...

- Put you down, embarrass or shame you?
- Call you names?
- Ignore you?
- Demand to know where you are every minute?
- Treat you as inferior?
- Purposefully embarrass you, often times in front of others?
- Not allow you to make decisions?
- Rarely validate your opinions?
- Threaten you?
- Tell you that you're crazy?
- Belittle your accomplishments, aspirations or plans?
- Forbid you from talking to or seeing your friends, family or coworkers?
- Keep you from sleeping?

- Accuse you of cheating or is possessively jealous?
- Cheat on you and then blame you for his or her behavior?
- Tell you that you will never find anyone better?
- Repeatedly point out your mistakes?
- Attempt to control what you wear?
- Threaten to hurt you, your children, your family or your pets?

Both men and women can be victims of emotional abuse. In a study by the National Institutes of Health, with 250 participants that ranged from age 18-61, researchers studied four aspects of emotional abuse in intimate partner relationships: isolation, sexual abuse, property damage and degradation.

Women experienced the highest rates of isolation (restricting a person's contact with family and friends or physically confining a person) and property damage, which is considered symbolic violence as well as a tool of financial control and abuse.

The study also found that younger people were more likely to experience emotional abuse than older people, and men's overall risk of emotional abuse may be increasing as a result of evolving gender roles, like men as homemakers and women as the breadwinner.

Reference:
https://www.domesticshelters.org/articles/identifying
-abuse/how-to-recognize-emotional-abuse

❧

Healthy Relationships

A healthy relationship means that both you and your partner are:

- **Communicative**. You talk openly about problems and listen to one another. You respect each other's opinions.
- **Respectful**. You value each other's opinions, feelings, and needs, and give each other the freedom to be yourself and be loved for who you are.
- **Trusting**. You believe what your partner has to say and don't feel the need to "prove" each other's trustworthiness.
- **Honest**. You're honest with each other but can still keep some things private.
- **Equal**. You make decisions together and hold each other to the same standards. You and your partner have equal say with regard to major decisions within the relationship. All partners have access to the resources they need.

- **Setting boundaries**. You enjoy spending time apart, alone, or with others. You respect each other's need for time and space apart. You communicate with each other about what you are and aren't comfortable with.

- **Practicing consent**. You talk openly about sexual and reproductive choices together. All partners always willingly consent to sexual activity and can safely discuss what you are and aren't comfortable with.

- **Parenting supportively**. All partners are able to parent in a way that they feel comfortable with. You communicate together about the needs of the child(ren), as well as the needs of the parents.

You may be in an unhealthy relationship if your partner is:

- **Non-communicative**. When problems arise, you fight or you don't discuss them at all.

- **Disrespectful**. You or your partner behave inconsiderately toward the other.

- **Not trusting**. You or your partner refuse to believe the other or feel entitled to invade their privacy.

- **Dishonest**. You or your partner lie, omit, or obscure facts.

- **Taking control**. You or your partner takes steps to suggest that one's desires and choices are more important than another's.

- **Isolating**. Your partner restricts your contact with other people, either in person or online.

- **Pressured into sexual activity**. One partner uses pressure or guilt against another to coerce them into sexual acts or reproductive choices.

- **Ignoring boundaries**. It's assumed or implied that only one partner is responsible for making informed decisions.

- **Unequal economically**. Finances aren't discussed. Financial decisions are made unilaterally or it's assumed that only one partner is in charge of finances.

Reference:
https://www.thehotline.org/resources/healthy-relationships/

❧

PTSD

Post-traumatic stress disorder (PTSD) is a disorder that develops in some people who have experienced a shocking, scary, or dangerous event.

It is natural to feel afraid during and after a traumatic situation. Fear triggers many split-second changes in the body to help defend against danger or to avoid it. This "fight-or-flight" response is a typical reaction meant to protect a person from harm. Nearly everyone will experience a range of reactions after trauma, yet most people recover from initial symptoms naturally. Those who continue to experience problems may be diagnosed with PTSD. People who have PTSD may feel stressed or frightened, even when they are not in danger.

Signs and Symptoms

While most but not all traumatized people experience short term symptoms, the majority do not develop ongoing (chronic) PTSD. Not everyone with PTSD has been through a dangerous event. Some experiences, like the sudden, unexpected death of a loved one, can also cause PTSD. Symptoms usually begin early, within 3 months of the traumatic incident, but sometimes they begin years afterward. Symptoms must last more than a month and be severe enough to interfere with relationships or work to be considered PTSD. The course of the illness varies. Some people recover within 6 months, while others have symptoms that last much longer. In some people, the condition becomes chronic.

A doctor who has experience helping people with mental illnesses, such as a psychiatrist or psychologist, can diagnose PTSD.

To be diagnosed with PTSD, an adult must have all of the following for at least 1 month:

- At least one re-experiencing symptom
- At least one avoidance symptom
- At least two arousal and reactivity symptoms
- At least two cognition and mood symptoms

Re-experiencing symptoms include:

- Flashbacks—reliving the trauma over and over, including physical symptoms like a racing heart or sweating
- Bad dreams
- Frightening thoughts

Re-experiencing symptoms may cause problems in a person's everyday routine. The symptoms can start from the person's own thoughts and feelings. Words, objects, or situations that are reminders of the event can also trigger re-experiencing symptoms.

Avoidance symptoms include:

- Staying away from places, events, or objects that are reminders of the traumatic experience

- Avoiding thoughts or feelings related to the traumatic event

Things that remind a person of the traumatic event can trigger avoidance symptoms. These symptoms may cause a person to change his or her personal routine. For example, after a bad car accident, a person who usually drives may avoid driving or riding in a car.

Arousal and reactivity symptoms include:

- Being easily startled
- Feeling tense or "on edge"
- Having difficulty sleeping
- Having angry outbursts

Arousal symptoms are usually constant, instead of being triggered by things that remind one of the traumatic events. These symptoms can make the person feel stressed and angry. They may make it hard to do daily tasks, such as sleeping, eating, or concentrating.

Cognition and mood symptoms include:

- Trouble remembering key features of the traumatic event

- Negative thoughts about oneself or the world
- Distorted feelings like guilt or blame
- Loss of interest in enjoyable activities

Cognition and mood symptoms can begin or worsen after the traumatic event, but are not due to injury or substance use. These symptoms can make the person feel alienated or detached from friends or family members.

It is natural to have some of these symptoms for a few weeks after a dangerous event. When the symptoms last more than a month, seriously affect one's ability to function, and are not due to substance use, medical illness, or anything except the event itself, they might be PTSD. Some people with PTSD don't show any symptoms for weeks or months. PTSD is often accompanied by depression, substance abuse, or one or more of the other **anxiety disorders**.

Reference:
https://www.nimh.nih.gov/health/topics/post-traumatic-stress-disorder-ptsd/

❦

Sexual Assault

Sexual assault can take many different forms, but one thing remains the same: it's never the victim's fault.

The term sexual assault refers to sexual contact or behavior that occurs without explicit consent of the victim. Some forms of sexual assault include:

- Attempted rape
- Fondling or unwanted sexual touching
- Forcing a victim to perform sexual acts, such as oral sex or penetrating the perpetrator's body
- Penetration of the victim's body, also known as rape

Rape is a form of sexual assault, but not all sexual assault is rape. The term rape is often used as a legal definition to specifically include sexual penetration without consent. For its Uniform Crime Reports, the FBI defines rape as "penetration, no matter how slight, of the vagina or anus with any body part or object, or oral penetration by a sex organ of another person, without the consent of the victim." To see how your state legally defines rape and other forms of sexual assault, visit RAINN's **State Law Database**.

Who are the perpetrators?

The majority of perpetrators are someone known to the victim. Approximately **eight out of 10 sexual assaults** are committed by someone known to the victim, such as in the case of **intimate partner sexual violence** or acquaintance rape.

The term "date rape" is sometimes used to refer to acquaintance rape. Perpetrators of acquaintance rape might be a date, but they could also be a classmate, a neighbor, a friend's significant other, or any number of different roles. It's important to remember that dating, instances of past intimacy, or other acts like kissing do not give someone consent for increased or continued sexual contact.

In other instances the victim may not know the perpetrator at all. This type of sexual violence is sometimes referred to as stranger rape. Stranger rape can occur in several different ways:

- Blitz sexual assault: when a perpetrator quickly and brutally assaults the victim with no prior contact, usually at night in a public place

- Contact sexual assault: when a perpetrator contacts the victim and tries to gain their trust by flirting, luring the victim to their car, or otherwise trying to coerce the victim into a situation where the sexual assault will occur

- Home invasion sexual assault: when a stranger breaks into the victim's home to commit the assault

Survivors of both stranger rape and acquaintance rape often blame themselves for behaving in a way that encouraged the perpetrator. It's important to remember that the victim is never to blame for the actions of a perpetrator.

To speak with someone who is trained to help, call the National Sexual Assault Hotline at 800.656.HOPE (4673) or chat online at online.rainn.org.

Reference: https://www.rainn.org/articles/sexual-assault

❧

Social Anxiety Disorder

People with social anxiety disorder have a general intense fear of, or anxiety toward, social or performance situations. They worry that actions or behaviors associated with their anxiety will be negatively evaluated by others, leading them to feel embarrassed. This worry often causes people with social anxiety to avoid social situations. Social anxiety disorder can manifest in a range of situations, such as within the workplace or the school environment.

Reference:
https://www.nimh.nih.gov/health/topics/anxiety-disorders/

❧

Suicide Prevention

Suicide is a major public health concern. Over 48,000 people died by suicide in the United States in 2018;

it is the **10th leading cause of death** overall. Suicide is complicated and tragic, but it is often preventable. Knowing the warning signs for suicide and how to get help can help save lives.

Signs and Symptoms

The behaviors listed below may be signs that someone is thinking about suicide.

- Talking about wanting to die or wanting to kill themselves

- Talking about feeling empty, hopeless, or having no reason to live

- Making a plan or looking for a way to kill themselves, such as searching for lethal methods online, stockpiling pills, or buying a gun

- Talking about great guilt or shame

- Talking about feeling trapped or feeling that there are no solutions

- Feeling unbearable pain (emotional pain or physical pain)

- Talking about being a burden to others

- Using alcohol or drugs more often

- Acting anxious or agitated

- Withdrawing from family and friends

- Changing eating and/or sleeping habits
- Showing rage or talking about seeking revenge
- Taking great risks that could lead to death, such as driving extremely fast
- Talking or thinking about death often
- Displaying extreme mood swings, suddenly changing from very sad to very calm or happy
- Giving away important possessions
- Saying goodbye to friends and family
- Putting affairs in order, making a will

If these warning signs apply to you or someone you know, get help as soon as possible, particularly if the behavior is new or has increased recently.

Here are the five steps you can take to be the one to help someone in emotional pain.

1. ASK: "Are you thinking about killing yourself?" It's not an easy question, but studies show that **asking at-risk individuals** if they are suicidal does not increase suicides or suicidal thoughts.

2. KEEP THEM SAFE: Reducing a suicidal person's access to highly lethal items or places is an important part of suicide prevention. While this is not always easy, asking if the at-risk person has a plan and

removing or disabling the lethal means can make a difference.

3. BE THERE: Listen carefully and learn what the individual is thinking and feeling. Research suggests **acknowledging and talking about suicide** may **reduce rather than increase** suicidal thoughts.

4. HELP THEM CONNECT: Save the National Suicide Prevention Lifeline's (1-800-273-TALK (8255)) and the Crisis Text Line's number (741741) in your phone, so it's there when you need it. You can also help make a connection with a trusted individual like a family member, friend, spiritual advisor, or mental health professional.

5. STAY CONNECTED: Staying in touch after a crisis or after being discharged from care can make a difference. **Studies have shown** the number of suicide deaths goes down when someone follows up with the at-risk person.

Reference:
https://www.nimh.nih.gov/health/topics/suicide-prevention/

❦

Made in the USA
Middletown, DE
14 July 2021

44129649R00150